SAINT PATRICK

Marian Broderick is a writer and editor who lives and works in London. She is second-generation Irish; her parents are from Donegal and Limerick. She spent every summer of her childhood in Ireland and has developed strong links with the place and the people.

Wild Irish Women: Extraordinary Lives from History proved hugely popular on publication in 2001 and the follow-up, *Bold, Brilliant and Bad: Irish Women from History*, was published in 2018.

SAINT PATRICK

LIFE, LEGEND AND LEGACY

MARIAN BRODERICK

THE O'BRIEN PRESS
DUBLIN

First published 2019 by The O'Brien Press Ltd,
12 Terenure Road East, Rathgar, D06 HD27, Dublin 6, Ireland.
Tel: +353 1 4923333; Fax: +353 1 4922777
E-mail: books@obrien.ie. Website: www.obrien.ie
The O'Brien Press is a member of Publishing Ireland.

ISBN: 978-1-84717-928-9

6 5 4 3 2 1
24 23 22 21 20 19

Printed and bound in Drukarnia Skleniarz, Poland.
The paper in this book is produced using pulp from managed forests.

General note on translations and place names:
The medieval texts referenced in this book were originally written in Latin or in Old
or Middle Irish; here they are translated into English and the translator credited. The
author is grateful to The O'Brien Press for permission to reproduce the translations of
George Otto Simms here. The English form of an Irish place name was part of the
process of colonisation and came much later than the original Irish name. They are
sometimes a transliteration, that is, rendered into English from Irish by sound. The
original Irish name is sometimes given in brackets with its translation.

Cover images
Front, top left © Failte Ireland/Tourism Ireland; top centre, centre left, centre right,
bottom right © Tourism Ireland; top right © Shutterstock; bottom left © Tourism
Ireland's Global Greening. Back cover images © Shutterstock

Published in

DUBLIN
UNESCO
City of Literature

ACKNOWLEDGEMENTS

Thanks to Dr Tim Campbell and the staff at The Saint Patrick Centre, Downpatrick, who were extremely helpful and informative. Also thanks to Sinéad Grace, Media and Public Relations Manager of Tourism Ireland, for all the Global Greening information.

Thanks to Ambassador Dan Mulhall for a timely song and being able to remember useful lyrics off the top of his head.

Thanks to Liz and Frank Cormack and Anne Flanagan for helping make my field trips not only possible but memorable. Thanks to Aidan and Clare Byrne, to Amanda Brace and to staff at the British Library for help with research. Thanks also to Patrick Lennon of Tourism Ireland for reading an early version of the manuscript.

Grateful thanks to Michael O'Brien, Ide ní Laoghaire, designer Emma Byrne and everyone at The O'Brien Press for bringing this project to life, especially my editor Aoife K. Walsh.

And the biggest thanks of all to Alfredo Cristiano and Conall Cristiano, who put up with my obsession for all things Patrician with such good grace.

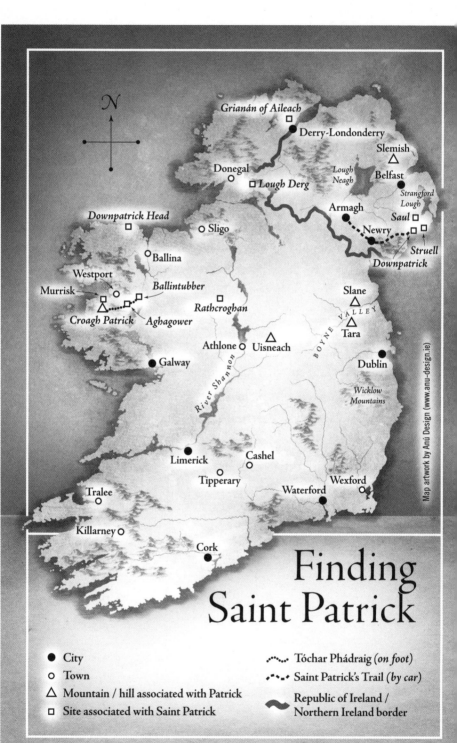

Finding Saint Patrick

- ● City
- ○ Town
- △ Mountain / hill associated with Patrick
- □ Site associated with Saint Patrick

- ⋯•⋯ Tóchar Phádraig (on foot)
- ◆⋯◆ Saint Patrick's Trail (by car)
- 〰 Republic of Ireland / Northern Ireland border

Map artwork by Anú Design (www.anu-design.ie)

CONTENTS

Introduction   page 09

Patrick Q&A   13

PART ONE: Ireland in Patrick's Time   21

PART TWO: Patrick's Story   77

PART THREE: Tall Tales from the Four Provinces   101

    Northern Light: Stories from Ulster   104
    Ends of the Earth: Stories from Connacht   122
    Valley of the Kings: Stories from Leinster 141
    From Myths to Monks: Stories from Munster   150

PART FOUR: The Greening of the World   163

Select Bibliography   195

Illustrations   200

Index of Place Names   201

INTRODUCTION

Slave, bishop and saint – it's fair to say that the man we call Patrick had an unusual life. Against the backdrop of the decline of the Roman Empire in fifth-century Europe, he ventured on many arduous journeys across land and sea to do the work he loved. But the most extraordinary journey of all occurred after his death, as his profile evolved from mere man to religious cult to global star.

All over the world, from California to Karachi, there are churches and cathedrals named for Patrick – there are two St Patrick's cathedrals each in the cities of Armagh and New York. There are schools, hospitals, clubs, streets, shopping centres and cul-de-sacs named for him.

In my own family there are eleven Patricks. My father and grandfather, uncles and first cousins have all been blessed with this, one of the most popular Irish boy's name ever. (They are rarely called Patrick in Ireland, though – there are too many of them. Instead, the multiple Patricks are known as Pat, Patie, Paddy, Pakie, Pádraig, Paudge or, in one memorable case, Phateen Phats!).

Then there is one of the world's biggest festivals, St Patrick's Day. Over the last century or so, the anniversary of the saint's death on 17 March has become a massive worldwide hooley, a byword for exuberant behaviour. With its parades, music, dancing, sports, green beer and commercial opportunities for the purveyors of eccentric headgear, it has become an international

9

phenomenon. It is a chance for everyone in the world to feel what it's like to be Irish for just one day. The next day they understand why it only happens once a year.

But what of the first Patrick and his work in Ireland? What we know for sure is that there was a real person named Patrick who was taken and enslaved by Irish raiders as a boy. We know he became a priest, then a missionary in Ireland, and that he left two written works behind him, copies of which remain: the autobiographical Confessio and his angry *Letter to Coroticus*.

The *Confessio* is the most important source we have, and the most tantalising. In it, Patrick talks about his kidnapping and his mission, plus some of the troubles he experienced in later life. The *Letter to Coroticus* is a tirade directed at a chieftain in Scotland, whose men had killed or sold into slavery a group of newly baptised Christians. From these writings we get glimpses of Patrick the man: stubborn, provocative, passionate, courageous.

These texts were copied by monks and widely distributed. Today, part of the *Confessio* exists in the 1000-year-old *Book of Armagh*, which resides in Trinity College, Dublin, and this fragment is the earliest surviving piece of writing in Ireland. Therefore, in a country of historians, storytellers and poets, Patrick can be considered our first historian, as he has the honour of being the author of the earliest recorded history we have.

Much of the rest of what we (think we) know about Patrick is based on the work of his earliest biographers, Irish clerics Muirchú and Tírechán. But these were rather imaginative works by the clerics intent on supporting the cult that was starting to flourish around the saint. The real places he visited, the miracles he performed and his age on death (120 years, according to one source) are all still shrouded in the mists of many centuries. We don't even know if Patrick was one man or two; there is a theory that the Patrick of the many tales we have inherited was preceded by a bishop named Palladius Patricius, and that the two lives have merged into one.

Some of the stories about Patrick may have more than a particle of truth in them, some are early examples of spin-doctoring by senior clerics in the early Irish church, and some are beautiful fairy tales, lovingly burnished over time by ordinary people. From a distance of fifteen centuries it is extremely difficult to know which is which, although Northern Ireland can certainly lay claim to the most concrete evidence of his life and death.

This book brings together the many different threads of these stories woven around Patrick. It looks at his life and his legacy, at the facts and the fiction, in order to understand how a small Irish cult grew into a story recognised around the world, and culminating in the global phenomenon that is St Patrick's Day. To do this, I gathered as many of the major facts and stories as possible from a wide variety of secondary sources. I investigated Patrick's own texts, as well as the seventh-century biographies of Muirchú and Tírechán. I travelled across the island of Ireland exploring Patrick's special places and pondering their significance for those who went before me so long ago.

This book is divided into four parts. Part One paints a picture of what Ireland, regarded in Patrick's time as the 'end of the earth', was like in the early medieval period (AD 500–1000).

Part Two, Patrick's Story, is a fictional account of what it might have been like for a teenager to be snatched from home one spring day in the early 400s and taken across the sea. It is told from his own perspective.

Part Three, Tall Tales from the Four Provinces, shares many of the legends of the beautiful and often secret places associated with Patrick's journey around Ireland.

Lastly, the Greening of the World, an initiative by Tourism Ireland, leaves us in no doubt that millions now commemorate the feast day of one man in a style that is distinctly twenty-first century with fun technology and colourful spectacle. And that man is St Patrick of Ireland, the bearded cleric in green with the tall hat and the crooked staff, the world's most recognisable patron saint.

PATRICK Q&A

WHERE WAS HE BORN?

This is a tricky one. In the *Confessio*, Patrick says he was born in a place called Bannaven Taburniae (or Banna Venta Burniae), which has proved impossible to locate. It is assumed to be on the west, northwest or southwest coast of Britain. This is reasonable given that the raiders came by sea, and the British west coast, which had been Romanised, was known to be a relatively rich area with good pickings.

So, Patrick's birthplace could also be in the Strathclyde area of Scotland, possibly Kilpatrick or Dumbarton, perhaps Cumbria in northwest England, Caerwent in Wales, the Severn Valley, or even the north coast of Cornwall. There is archaeological evidence of Irish raiders and even Irish settlers in all these places, and at the time of Patrick's birth in the late fourth century, these coasts were no longer defended by the Romans.

A more far-fetched theory suggests that Patrick might not have been born in Britain at all, but in Brittany, France. There is a tradition there that he was kidnapped from the area around the Château de Bonaban (sounds similar to Bannaven!), which is in La Gouesnière, a commune in the Ille-et-Vilaine department of Brittany in northwest France. In ancient sources written after Patrick's lifetime, there is often a confusion in the names for 'Britain' and 'Brittany', and this fuelled the speculation.

WHEN WAS HE BORN?

Circa AD 385 is as close as we can get to a birth year for Patrick. This was around the time Christianity became the official religion of the Roman Empire, which extended from Scotland in the north to Africa in the south, and Spain in the west to Croatia in the east. The possibility that there were two Patricks (see page 19), one after the other, obviously affects birth and death dates.

WHO WERE HIS FAMILY?

One ancient theory maintains Patrick was of royal blood. He does tell us in the *Confessio* that his father was called Calpurnius and his grandfather Potitus. Some sources say that Calpurnius was a prince, originally from the royal family of a northern tribe in the Kingdom of Strathclyde. Patrick himself says that his father was a decurion, or deacon, with a small estate.

Unfortunately, Patrick says nothing of his mother in the *Confessio*. It was later said that she was 'of the Franks', that is, French, and went by the name Concessa. She was also said to be the niece of St Martin of Tours – another French connection. Legends surrounding Patrick say that he had many sisters, including St Dererca, who had eighteen sons. Some of Patrick's siblings, nieces and nephews came to work for him in Ireland.

DID YOU KNOW?

Patrick's birth name is unknown but may have been Maewyn Succat.
'Patrick' was the name he chose upon becoming a priest.

WHERE IN IRELAND WAS HE A SLAVE?

This one is a little controversial. Northern Ireland 'own' Patrick, and the official line is that he served his slavery, a common practice at the time, on Slemish Mountain, County Antrim. However, the only place in Ireland he ever mentions in the *Confessio* is 'Silva Focluti by the western sea', or the Woods of Foclut, and he says that this is where he slaved. It is possible that this may be an area today known as Foghill, which lies in the once densely wooded region along Killala Bay on the coast of Mayo.

Slemish Mountain, County Antrim, with hawthorn tree in the foreground

HOW DID HE ESCAPE?

Around age thirty, slaves were often given their freedom because they were past their best as workers, and might prove expensive to support. Instead, they were expected to leave and become self-sufficient farmers.

But Patrick didn't wait for this to happen; one day he simply ran away.

In the *Confessio*, Patrick says his escape wasn't straightforward. After running away and making his way across Ireland on foot, he managed to find passage aboard a ship, which sailed for three days, went off course, and landed in a deserted, barren place. He and the crew wandered for several weeks and nearly starved. They were saved by prayer and the timely appearance of a herd of pigs. These they killed and ate, before finally finding a settlement.

Historians have always argued that these wanderings were a metaphor, because there was no such deserted place near Ireland or Britain. However, recent studies have shown that, instead of landing in Scotland or the west coast of Britain as intended, Patrick and the crew might have landed on the coast of modern Brittany in France. Three days in a hide boat could get you there from Ireland. The landscape was densely wooded hills with few pathways, and easy to get lost in. More importantly, there was a peasants' revolt in AD 409, followed by a famine. This may explain both the lack of food and the deserted farmsteads; much of the Romanised population would have left at the same time as the Romans themselves pulled back and retreated into Italy to regroup. The few people that remained doubtless hid from any newcomers, likely fearing they were Germanic scouting parties preparing to invade or kidnap.

WHERE DID HE GO AFTER HIS ESCAPE?

After Patrick's escape, there's a period of around twenty-three years we can only guess at. In the *Confessio*, he says he spent some time with his family and then received a vision that prompted him to become ordained, so he took off for France, where there was a number of well-known Christian communities. He may have studied for some years with St Martin of Tours (316/336–397) in the Loire Valley. He is also said to have been a pupil of St Germanus of Auxerre (c. 378–448). As we can see from the dates, one of those could be true, but not both.

WHY DID HE RETURN TO IRELAND?

After his escape from slavery, Patrick continued to experience prophetic dreams, visions and voices. One night while visiting his family, he dreamed of a man named Victoricus, the only other person named in the *Confessio*. Victoricus stood before him, waving letters that contained a life-changing message: the 'cry of the Irish'. The people were begging Patrick to come back and 'walk among them once more'.

WHO WAS WITH HIM?

Patrick did not come back to Ireland alone. Tírechán claims he was consecrated a bishop when he came (though this has been disputed by later scholarship), and so would have had servants and an entourage. In fact, his twenty-four regular helpers included a Brehon (lawyer/judge), a psalmist, a bell ringer, a cook, a brewer, a charioteer, a woodman, a strong man, two waiters, three smiths, three artists, three embroiderers (all women), several nephews and a scribe named Brogan. It is interesting to note that, until the later medieval period, Christian priests were not forbidden to marry, so long as they didn't leave church property to their spouses. Some stories about Patrick maintain that he was married and that his wife was named Sheelagh. This belief died out in Ireland but persisted in parts of America, Australia and Canada, where the day after St Patrick's Day is still known as Sheelagh's Day.

WHEN AND WHERE DID HE DIE?

It would seem that Patrick had the constitution of an ox and lived until he was an old man. He may have died in c. 460, not long after writing the *Confessio*, although some scholars place his death much later in the fifth century. His death is commemmorated in the Church on 17 March.

Patrick may have died in either Saul or Downpatrick (both in County Down); later stories said St Tassach (d. 470) presided over his deathbed (see Raholp, page 110). As a really important holy figure, with the beginnings of a cult already gathering around him, there was likely to be a tussle over his earthly remains, but today many believe that most of him is buried in Downpatrick.

A PACK OF PATS

Patrick wasn't the only missionary in Ireland in the fifth century. He possibly wasn't even the only Patrick. His was not an uncommon name of Romanised and/or ordained men from Britain and across Europe. In the British Isles there was at least one other contemporary missionary known as 'Sen Patrick' or 'Patrick the Elder'. There was also a French Patrick, connected with a monastery at Nevers. The activities of the several Patricks may have become conflated over time. For example, it may be the French Patrick's relics that were housed at Glastonbury, which led to the idea that Patrick of Ireland was buried there.

We do know that in 431 Pope Celestine I sent a bishop named Palladius to Ireland from Gaul. In his 1942 book, *The Two Patricks*, Thomas F. O'Rahilly maintains that Palladius (or Patricius Palladius as he is called in the *Book of Armagh*, a ninth-century collection of texts) did arrive in Ireland around that date, and that the widely held belief that he lasted only a year or two is false. O'Rahilly claims Palladius completed a lifetime's work and died around 457 or 460. At this point, another cleric, 'Patricius Secundus', arrived from Britain to build on his predecessor's mission. It is this second Patrick that we think of as Ireland's saint. He travelled and worked across Ireland until his own death in the 490s. Crucially, says O'Rahilly, it was he who was the writer of the *Confessio* and the *Letter to Coroticus*, and therefore it was he who became the focus of the national cult.

PART ONE

IRELAND IN PATRICK'S TIME

Fifth-century Ireland enjoyed a pagan, Celtic culture. It was polytheistic, featuring many deities, although by the 530s there were already small pockets of Christianity in the south of Ireland. Centuries-old practices, led by druids, included worshipping the gods of natural features, such as freshwater springs and trees, sacrificing animals and humans, and forecasting the future. Entirely dependent on a rich oral tradition, Ireland was a war-like, hierarchical society with strict rules, where personal attributes, such as physical bravery, skill in healing, hospitality and story-telling, were prized by the Celts.

Patrick knew all this when he arrived and he used this knowledge to push his own message home. He worked within the status quo where he could, taking over existing sacred sites and turning chieftains into bishops. But as we will see, he was also willing to face down any opposition he met.

For centuries after Patrick, Christianity and paganism co-existed in Ireland, and features of pagan life became incorporated into stories about Patrick. For our understanding of him today, we have to thank two of his earliest biographers, Muirchú and Tírechán, who wrote about him in the seventh century, as well as Patrick's own writings, the *Confessio* and the *Letter to Coroticus*. Because of them and the growth of the Patrician cult, Patrick's work, life and death went from being a mere historical event, to a well-loved Irish legend, to an international legacy.

Opposite: The water from a sacred spring was commonly believed to cure blindness, as shown in this 1869 print.

IRELAND'S VIPS

Long, long ago, beyond the misty space
Of twice a thousand years,
In Erin old there dwelt a mighty race
Taller than Roman spears...

The Celts, Thomas D'Arcy McGee

The Ireland Patrick came to was organised in a rigid class system, although there was no central state authority and everybody lived within clans on ancestral tribal land. Every person in every clan in the country had their place in society, from slave to king. The concept of honour was central, as was kinship and the strength of an oath.

The system was a pyramid. The majority at the bottom were unfree men and women. Above them were the 'cowmen', or farmers, who headed a household and rented a few cattle from their immediate superior, the tribal chieftain. This chieftain presided over his clan, but he paid homage to an under-king (for example, the kings of Thomond and of Ossory). The under-kings paid homage to provincial kings, or over-kings, who might lay claim to most of a province (such as the kings of Ulster and of Cashel). Finally, at the apex of the pyramid, there was the high king, or ardrí. High Kings were inaugurated at the Hill of Tara in County Meath in the centuries before and after Patrick's arrival, and they expected support, subservience and cattle from all the provincial kings under them.

Chieftains and kings employed high-status poets and druids. Poets were responsible for immortalising clan leaders in the oral tradition, and druids were responsible for the spiritual life of the clan. The roles required years of training and a phenomenal memory; druids learned all the rituals for how to contact the Otherworld, placate the gods and protect the people.

BREHON MARRIAGE

The Brehon Code of Ireland was a sophisticated legal system that existed for up to two thousand years before Christianity. Memorised by special lawyers known as brehons, they began to be written down and changed after Patrick's arrival.

Patrick got involved in trying to stamp out many aspects of the laws. Druids were his arch enemies and he banned their activities, such as sacrifices to the pagan gods. He also curtailed the activities of bards (although he did allow them still to practise, recognising the enormous talent and years of hard work that went into the feats of memory for which they were famous).

But he failed miserably when he tried to control Irish marriages.

The church idea of 'one husband, one wife' was not the Irish way in the fifth century. There were at least nine different types of marriages available – multiple marriages, cousin marriages, temporary marriages, marriages by abduction. It was common for a man to have a main or first wife, a second wife, and sometimes even a third wife.

Women had more rights in Ireland than in the rest of Europe at the time – and certainly more than British women as late as the nineteenth century. Divorce was acceptable, and so was temporary marriage, which a woman could leave after a year and a day, with no blame on either side. Each woman brought her own property, which she took with her if she left the marriage, plus any profit she made. All the wives' children were legitimate children and could inherit. Taking more than one husband at a time, however, was not an option open to women.

None of this was to the liking of the Pope and the wider church but, despite Patrick's efforts, Brehon marriage customs were to continue in many regions for another thousand years until the Elizabethan reconquest of Ireland in the sixteenth century.

DID YOU KNOW?

Green, now universally associated with St Patrick's Day, was once considered unlucky because it was linked with fairies. Until recently, it was very unlucky in Ireland to get married in green.

RELIGION, PAGAN-STYLE

The druid's altar and the druid's deed
We scarce can trace,
There is not an undisputed deed
of all your race...

The Celts, Thomas D'Arcy McGee

The religious culture that Patrick found in Ireland was nature-based with many gods. It explained how the world had come into being, how to survive its apparent randomness and cruelty and how to improve your own luck.

In the pagan belief system, the Ancient Ones dominated different aspects of life: Lugh, the lord of light; Crom, the earth father, and the goddesses Macha, Tailte and Danu to name but a few. The gods and goddesses haunted special locations (those liminal or threshold areas often called 'thin places' in later folklore) in mountains, forests, bogs and springs, and it was well known that, at any moment, one of them might appear in any sort of mood. They could help you, make you rich, or ensure your victory against a rival tribe. But they could harm you too. They could send you bad weather. They could make your cows run dry, your crops fail. They could destroy your family. They could annihilate your whole clan.

Grange Stone Circle, County Limerick

The druids explained the signs of anger or approval, and they led the chieftain and his clan in time-honoured, nature-centred customs in stone circles and oak groves at certain times of the year, such as at midsummer and midwinter. They led celebrations during the four great fire festivals of the year, which were known as Imbolc (early spring), Bealtaine (early summer), Lughnasa (late summer) and Samhain (late autumn).

Imbolc – 1 February during lambing time.	This celebration of the end of winter and the longer days to come was taken over by the Christian feast day of St Brigid, another of Ireland's patron saints, who replaced an earlier pagan fertility goddess of the same name.
Bealtaine – 1 May or May Day.	Traditionally a time when young men and women's fancy turns lightly to thoughts of love. The bilberry is picked, and its white blossom is given as love tokens.
Lughnasa – late July/early August.	This 'first fruits' festival is still celebrated on Garland or Reek Sunday, when pilgrims ascend Croagh Patrick. Neolithic and Bronze Age people would have used this time of year to pay homage to their harvest gods.
Samhain – 31 October.	A spooky 'turn of the year' festival, which was imported to America and became Halloween. People traditionally tell ghost stories, play games and forecast the future.

DID YOU KNOW?

Baal was an ancient sun god. Baal tinne (the fire of Baal) is the root of the important spring fire festival of Bealtaine.

SACRIFICING HUMANS

Pagan people gave gifts to their gods. Usually this was food, drink, precious metals and other goods. But sometimes the gods required the ultimate sacrifice – human life. There are now many examples of 'bog bodies' in the archaeological record of Ireland and northwest Europe, human bodies that have been mummified in the cool, oxygen-free environment of the peat bog. Irish examples include Old Croghan Man and Clonycavan man, found in County Meath, and Cashel Man, found in County Laois. These individuals, specially chosen because of their high, even kingly status, were given a ritual meal, such as sloe berries. They were then taken to the marshy threshold between two worlds, the bog being neither land nor water. There they were killed in a ferocious and ritual manner – 'over-killed' in fact. According to the evidence, their injuries included holes cut through their arms, nipples sliced off, and axe wounds to the head. Their bodies were then left where they fell as a gift for the gods.

One theory suggests that the nipple-slicing injuries on Clonycavan Man and Old Croghan Man shows that they were failed candidates for kingship; nipple-sucking a king was a submissive gesture in Iron Age Ireland.

Worse still was the sacrifice of 'firstlings', that is, firstborn calves, lambs – and babies. Hideous though it is to contemplate now, there was a time when healthy infants, the most precious offering of all, would be sacrificed to ensure the survival of the whole tribe.

It was into this world that Patrick came with his news that

This Irish peat bog shows clearly where turf has been cut.

there were not many gods, but only One. Certainly this One needed placating just as the many gods had, but the difference was that it was He who had made the ultimate sacrifice. He had sent His own child to die for the people. Now the people owed Him their love, their fear and their loyalty.

And what did they get in return? According to Patrick, the greatest reward of all – everlasting life.

BARDS: THE PEOPLE'S POETS

Druids, bards, brehons and *ollamhs* (teachers) made up a professional class of poets near the top of Gaelic society. It required twenty years of study to become a member of this class.

The use of poetry was incredibly important to the Celts of Patrick's time when Ireland was a wholly oral culture, and poetry was used to memorise family records and stories. Every royal house had a resident bard. If it was the druid's job to mediate between this world and the Otherworld, it was the bard's job to memorise and retell legends about that Otherworld, as well as the legendary exploits of their employer and their employer's ancestors. While the coming of Christianity stripped druids of much of their power, bards retained their high and special status into the seventeenth century. Their verses, when they were turned to the purpose of satirising their patron's enemies, could be so powerful they could result in death.

After he won over the High King Loegaire (see page 58), Patrick banned most of the old bardic ways, including the act of prophecy. But he did appreciate the years of study and skill that went into the oral tradition of memorising verse so he allowed bards to make music and rhyme, and to keep 350 of their stories. Ironically, this actually ensured the survival of the pagan gods in Irish culture. And this is how stories of Manannán mac Lir (god of the sea), Dagda (god of music), Danu (Mother Earth), Lugh of the Long Arm (god of light), the Morrigan (goddess of destruction) and Crom Cruaich (Father Earth and later god of the harvest) have come down to the present day. The bards also passed on stories about the giants that had inhabited Ireland before the Celts, the Fir Bolg, the coming of the Milesians, and the famous heroes, Fionn mac Cumhall and Cú Chulainn.

A brehon, after whom the Brehon Code is named, is often referred to as a type of judge or lawyer because the Code he memorised and shared with others was largely to do with fines levied and the treatment of criminals and victims. Pre-Christian Celtic justice was restorative – that is, how a crime could be repaid in cattle or other goods – and the Code was based on long years of precedent. The brehon had the power to hand down judgements, but he could only do this because he had spent many years training his memory to learn all the legal judgements of the past, similar to a bard. Brehons had to qualify as ollamhs, first, but to do either of these jobs he also had to become a bard, that is, gain a degree in poetry.

SACRED WATERS AND OTHER 'THIN PLACES'

Because the Celts believed in an Otherworld, just as much as Christians believed in an Afterlife, they also knew of ways to enter it. These access points were remembered in local folklore, which unconsciously referred to much earlier pagan practices, as 'thin places' – special thresholds where the veil between our world and the Otherworld could be lifted.

Thin places included bogland, mountain-tops, freshwater springs and wells, and sacred trees and rocks. When Patrick and his successors came, they took over these ancient pagan power centres to practice Christianity.

According to one estimate, there are some 3,000 holy wells in Ireland. They are usually freshwater springs where people come to pray and leave simple offerings. To say they date from pre-Christian times is putting it mildly; wells are central to the oldest forms of spiritual worship in Ireland. The Irish for well, fountain or spring is 'tobar', so many settlements by holy wells carry a version of the word in the name (tobber, tubber).

For the pagans of Ireland, water was often associated with femaleness. The Boyne River is named after the goddess Boann,

Taking the waters at a holy well and shrine, Lough Gill,
County Sligo, c. 1901

Rapids on the Shannon, County Limerick

and the Shannon River is named for a mythical woman named Sionann. It is thought that many of the springs and wells of the pre-Christian era were devoted to pagan goddesses, such as Brigid (see page 145).

Pagan belief held that water was as a threshold between the natural and supernatural worlds. Therefore when people wanted to communicate with supernatural beings in times of trouble or hope, they threw valued objects into the water. That is why so many of the earliest archaeological finds are discovered in or near ancient wells, springs or boglands: they were attempts by people to contact the Otherworld they were certain lay on the other side.

PAGAN TO CHRISTIAN

After Christianity's arrival, the ancient wells lost their connection with pagan goddesses. One by one, Christian stories became attached to them instead, so that wells retained their specialness by being associated with saints rather than gods. Today Brigid, the fifth-century saint, is the patron of many of the wells that had been linked with her much older, pagan counterpart of the same name.

Much merrymaking would likely have taken place as part of the ritual around holy wells from the pre-Christian era through to the early and medieval Christian years but, over time, this was replaced with the more penitential activity known as Stations, a combination of prayers and walking commemorating the journey of Christ to the cross.

Patrick's use of the wells around Ireland is clear; he harnessed the pagan power of the sacred waters to baptise new Christians, bestowing an extra holiness to an already powerful magnet for pilgrims. The earliest churches were nearly always built near a spring so that today the majority of holy wells are to be found near ancient churches and graveyards.

WARTS AND ALL

A well often had curative powers over particular ailments, particularly eye infections and warts. And the names given to the wells sometimes reflect those illnesses: Tobar na Súl (the Eye Well), Tobar na Plá (the Well of the Plague), Tobar na nGealt (the Well of the Insane). At these wells it was customary to drink the water, bathe the diseased part of the body or wash it with a cloth. The cloth was then attached to a nearby rag tree as a votive offering. The cloth was often red as it was believed the colour red repelled the power of evil spirits. As the rag rotted away, so too did the illness.

Opposite: St Patrick's Well, Downpatrick, County Down

The many St Patrick's wells in Ireland vary in appearance and decoration, from simple stone arrangements, such as at Holywell, Belcoo, County Fermanagh, to modern bronze statues of the saint himself, such as at Ballintubber Abbey in County Mayo.

PENAL TIMES AND BEYOND

The springs from which Patrick and the early saints of Ireland took water were seen as places of pilgrimage. But it was only when Catholic practices were suppressed during Penal Times (1697–1829) that large numbers began to assemble in secret for mass at holy wells or remote places on hillsides where there might be a large rock that could be used as an altar. Later these became known as mass rocks.

ST PATRICK'S WELLS AROUND IRELAND

Following is a list, in alphabetical order and by no means exhaustive, of some of the more interesting St Patrick's wells in the island of Ireland.

Ardfert, County Kerry

This well, in Tubrid More, is also known as Tobar na Molt (Well of the Wethers). It acquired this unusual name during

Penal Times. The authorities' tracker dogs were closing in on the people attending mass near the well, when three wethers (castrated rams) jumped out and drew the dogs away. The site actually has more links with the beloved and local St Ita, than with Patrick.

Carrigatogher, Ballywilliam, County Tipperary

Folklore records how locals visited this well every Saturday for its curative powers. There are said to be marks on it known as St Patrick's Fingers.

Clonmel, County Tipperary

One of the largest holy wells in Ireland, local legend has it that Patrick carried out many baptisms here. There is a fifth-century Celtic cross in the middle of it.

Croghan Hill, County Offaly

Near to Croghan Hill is a holy well and people say if the *bullán* (bullaun) stone is taken away, it will magically return. A bullaun is a cup-shaped depression in rock, sometimes filled with water or stones, and it is often associated with pre-Christian ritual, such as drinking the water for a cure or turning the stones for a curse. Another local custom has it that one may not boil water from this well. On Croghan Hill itself the custom was to light the gorse bushes and drive cattle through them in a pre-Christian purification ritual. Latterly the same ritual took place on St Patrick's Day.

Opposite: Age Celtic cross in St Patrick's Well, Clonmel, County Tipperary

Duncrun (Dun Cruithne), County Derry-Londonderry

The first church on this hillside overlooking the sea was originally named after St Cadan (Teampall Chadáin, meaning Cadan's church), who was a follower of Patrick. Over time, the name became corrupted from St Cadan to St Aidan, to whom a later thirteenth-century church was dedicated. There is a holy well nearby and the water from the well is said to heal any sickness when applied to the relevant body part. Cadan's grave is said to lie under the gable of the medieval ruins of the church, where there is a cross slab embedded in the ground.

Foghill, County Mayo

On the stunning Mayo coast lies the parish of Lacken and the small rural area, or townland, of Foghill. This tiny place is significant because Patrick wrote that when he was a slave he tended sheep in 'the Wood of Foclut by the western sea'. This is one of the very few times he mentions any place by name in his writing and it is the only time he mentions a place in Ireland. Today the closest most scholars can come to this location is Foghill. Here there is a St Patrick's Well, and a statue commissioned by the local people in 1936 'in honour of St Patrick', which still stands. To do the Stations here, the custom is to circle three mounds of earth at the site in a clockwise direction, while reciting prayers, and drinking water from the holy well.

Glaspatrick, County Mayo

Next to the very significant site, Croagh Patrick, is the townland of Glaspatrick, where there are the remains of a church, probably twelfth century, and a pre-Christian holy well. The area takes its name from the nearby stream, Glais Phádraig (Patrick's Stream). One of Patrick's charioteers, a man named Totmáel, is said to have died in the area and to have been buried at this site.

Kilgeever, County Mayo

A church, Cill Iomhair, was founded here by St Iomhair after St Patrick had visited Croagh Patrick. The present ruins are twelfth or thirteenth century. There is a holy well named after Patrick and some cross slabs on the site, as well as a pilgrimage Station.

Killeter, County Tyrone

Here the holy well is known locally as Tober Patrick. Tradition has it that Patrick stopped here to quench his thirst after leaving 'Patrick's Purgatory' at Lough Derg, County Donegal (see page 118). The monastic site dates from the sixth century with only a small section of wall remaining now.

Kill na Greina, County Cork

Meaning 'Church of the Sun', local tradition says there was once a 'druid temple' or a pagan stone circle here – plus a miraculous well. Inside the well was a prophesying woman known as *ban na naomha* (holy woman). The story goes that when Patrick came across this sacred spot he was horrified and cursed the area, turning it overnight into a marsh. Lady Jane Wilde (mother of Oscar), who collected this story in her book, *Ancient Legends, Mystic Charms and Superstitions of Ireland*, wrote that a farmer drained the marsh in the late 1700s and uncovered the stone circle and the well. After its rediscovery,

Opposite: Kilgeever holy well, County Mayo

pilgrims began to visit. They went around the well nine times, leaving a white stone on it as an offering. Eventually a regular festival, known as a 'pattern day' (see page 132), grew up around the well, but the festivities became too raucous for the taste of local clerics and the custom was banned.

DID YOU KNOW?

According to Lady Jane Wilde, the Bealtaine custom of extinguishing domestic fires and rekindling them from a sacred fire on a hill came to Ireland from Persia (present-day Iran).

Magherakeel, County Tyrone

The legend of this well is that on the way back from Lough Derg, where he had been for Lent, Patrick stopped here and quenched his thirst. The water is said to cure toothache.

Mungret, County Limerick

The well associated with Patrick here has since disappeared. Local people used to 'do the rounds' here, that is, perform the Stations and take home water from the well to sick relatives. But one day a strange woman washed clothes in the well, and the well lost its virtue.

Straffan, County Kildare

The holy well near the chapel here has a tradition that boys throw turf at each other on St Patrick's Day. The region has many prehistoric features, and one of them, now called St Patrick's Hill, was the location of ancient tribal assemblies of old.

Tawnagh West, County Clare

This site has an ancient ritual bath, known as St Patrick's Well, where pilgrims used to wash. Incidentally, there is another Tawnagh with a St Patrick's Well in County Sligo.

Tobberpatrick, Strand Head, Portstewart, County Derry-Londonderry

By the beaches of the northern coast of Portstewart, there is a St Patrick's Well, also known as Tobberpatrick. Archaeology shows that this well was used by prehistoric groups that settled the area. Over time it became a sacred well, before being Christianised by Patrick.

The medieval pilgrimages that happened here were penitential in nature with much scourging and fasting and general suffering. Gradually, over centuries, this penitential aspect was dropped and the social aspect became more important. Today this site still sees large, regular gatherings but no longer in pilgrimage. Instead it plays host to a summer fair, held on the last Monday in August.

Trinity College, corner of Nassau and Dawson streets, Dublin

At the site of the well in the grounds of Trinity College, Patrick struck the ground with his staff and water bubbled to the surface. The well gave the street its older name in Irish, Sráid Thobar Phádraig (street of St Patrick's Well), before it was changed to Nassau as a compliment King William III of England (known in Ireland and Scotland as 'King Billy'). It dried up in 1729 when local building work altered the water table, but now has water in it once again.

Tullaghan, near Corbeg, County Leitrim

This is a site with not one but two holy wells: Tobar Phádraig (Patrick's Well) and the unusually named Tobar an Bhearrtha (Well of the Shaving). The wells were famous for eye cures. There is a pilgrimage to the wells every St Patrick's Day, when participants are invited to drink the water.

There are also St Patrick's Wells at Carna, Mullaghorne, County Cavan; Ballyshannon (near ruins of Assaroe Abbey), County Donegal; Sheeplands East, Lecale, County Down; Ballymurphy Road, Tullow, County Carlow; at Patrickswell, Rathvilly, County Carlow and Toberpatrick, County Fermanagh, near the Glen mass rock. Locations for St Patrick's Wells in County Meath include Tobar Patraic, near Ardmulchan, and Carlanstown, near Kilbeg. And others in Connacht include St Patrick's Wells in Mám Éan (Maumeen), County Galway; Cartron, Granard, County Longford; Kilcorkey parish, County Roscommon; Cluain Patrick, Athleague, County Roscommon and Dromard and Aughris, County Sligo.

NATIVE TREES

There is on the north side of the glen,
If we were both brought there,
A tree whose berries are good to taste,
Which is named the Wry Rowan.
If you were nine days without food,
I tell you, it is no foolish thought,
It would relieve your dryness and your thirst,
When you would see the colour of the berries …

Extract from *The Wry Rowan*,
ninth-century poem, translated by Eoin MacNeill

Ireland, like Britain, was largely covered with dense forest in Patrick's time. For the Celts, trees were special. They had magic properties, and were venerated by druids. Each tribe had a tree species or even an individual tree that it held sacred.

The druids' sacred trees included willow, hazel, hawthorn, oak and rowan (mountain ash). Rowan was said to confer the gift of prophecy; the evergreen yew was associated with everlasting life. Hawthorn (whitethorn) is traditionally associated with the *sídhe* (fairies) in Irish tradition, hence its alternative name, the fairy thorn. It is also commonly linked with Patrick and is often called 'Patrick's tree'.

Druids fed permitted sacred wood into fires during the festivals of Bealtaine and Samhain to help them predict the future. A thirteenth-century poem outlines tree lore:

The graceful tree with the berries, the wizard's tree, the rowan,
  burn;
But spare the limber tree; burn not the slender hazel.
The noble willow burn not, a tree sacred to poems ...

The main expression of tree worship in modern times is the use of the rag tree, often found near holy wells. When people visit, they may bring a cloth, dip it into the holy well's water and tie it to the nearby tree with a request – either to a saint or to the fairies, depending on their belief system. If the request is for the cure of sickness, as the cloth rots away, so does the illness disappear.

Rag tree near Hill of Tara, County Meath

DID YOU KNOW?

In folklore, during Bealtaine, fairies had much power over children, cattle, butter and milk. To ward off the threat, a lump of spent coal would be placed under the cradle or the churn.

SACRED HEIGHTS

Mountains were an obvious and special feature in any landscape. Mountaintops gave a view of the surrounding country and were therefore defensible but, more importantly, they were physically far enough above and away from the normal daily existence of the lowlands to be a special space for communing with the fickle gods. From Neolithic times they were used for rituals and festivals, and even assisted in understanding solar cycles at certain times of the year (see Boheh Stone, page 132). By Patrick's day, they were special places used as inauguration sites for royalty and gathering places for traditional assemblies, which were held every three years and where attendance was compulsory.

Patrick identified several mountains and hills that were sacred in Ireland in his time:

- Croagh Patrick, County Mayo
- Benbulben, County Sligo
- Slieve Beagh, counties Monaghan, Fermanagh and Tyrone
- Slieve League, County Donegal
- Slieve Donard, County Down
- Cashel, County Tipperary

There were existing pagan legends associated with some of these. Benbulben was the scene of mortal combat between Fionn mac Cumhaill and Diarmuid over the beautiful Gráinne; later it became linked with the story of another fight – this time between two saints, Columba and Finnian.

Slieve Donard gets its name from St Dónairt, who was put in place by Patrick to guard the surrounding area from the hilltop. Before that it was named Slieve Slainge, after the mythical first physician in Ireland. But the most famous mountain of all is Croagh Patrick, which lost its pagan name of Cruachán Aigle and became known as Croagh Patrick, or Patrick's Mountain, sometime after 441, when the saint spent Lent there.

View of Croagh Patrick over Clew Bay

CROAGH PATRICK

And Patrick proceeded to Mons Aigli [Croagh Patrick], intending to
fast for 40 days and 40 nights, following the example of
Moses, Elias and Christ ...
Book of Armagh

Once known as Cruachán Aigle, and now also known locally
as The Reek, this mountain on the south side of Clew Bay in
County Mayo is now probably the most famous site associated
with Patrick and the most popular Patrician pilgrimage site in
Ireland.

But its importance as a place of worship goes back as far as
3,000 BC, long before Patrick's arrival, when Stone Age humans
gathered on the summit to worship the life-giving sun. Neolithic art can still be seen on a rock, now known as St Patrick's
Chair, which is along the path to the top.

Much later, the Celts used it as a gathering site for the
late-summer festival of Lughnasa, named for Lugh, the god of
harvest, and many stories tell that the earliest Irish god of fertility, Crom Cruaich (and a later version known as Crom Dubh),
was worshipped here. Still on the theme of fertility, it is said that
women would spend the night on the mountain to encourage a
pregnancy.

In 441, Patrick completed a Lenten ritual of penance at the top
of this mountain. The legends are well-known: he fasted for forty
days and nights, he was assailed by demons, he banished Ireland's

Opposite: Kildangan standing stones aligned with Croagh Patrick

St Patrick banishing snakes from Ireland

snakes into the lough below. One common folk legend tells how he made friends with Crom Cruaich himself and entered into friendly competition with him, resulting in the saint walking away with the god's prize bull.

The last Sunday of July is known as Crom Dubh Sunday (or, in Irish, Domhnach Chrom Dubh), after the vanquished god, and also as Reek Sunday. On this day, thousands of hikers, from the locality and from abroad, ascend Croagh Patrick. Some honour the memory of Patrick by climbing the mountainside barefoot, as an act of penance. And some honour the sun, as the most ancient worshippers did. Warning: this climb is not for the faint-hearted!

THE STATIONS: WHAT ARE THEY AND HOW ARE THEY PERFORMED?

In modern times, a ritual known as 'the Stations' is often performed on pilgrimages and around holy wells. This is a procession that symbolises the last journey of Jesus, and involves stopping at specific places for prayer and meditation. The idea of a circular journey at special times of the year, and the use of sacred incantations, all have their roots in pagan practice.

There are three Stations along the pilgrimage route to the summit of Croagh Patrick, each of which has a sign with instructions for the proper rituals and prayers. The Stations are as follows:

- First Station (Leacht Benáin, base of the mountain): walk seven times around this mound of stones while saying seven Our Fathers, seven Hail Marys and one Creed.
- Second Station (Summit): kneel near the chapel and say seven Our Fathers, seven Hail Marys and one Creed. Walk fifteen times around the chapel while saying fifteen Our Fathers and fifteen Hail Marys. Walk seven times around Leaba Phádraig (Patrick's Bed) saying seven Our Fathers, seven Hail Marys and one Creed.

- Third Station (Reilig Mhuire): walk seven times around each mound of stones saying seven Our Fathers, seven Hail Marys and one Creed. Walk seven times around the whole enclosure of Reilig Mhuire praying.

Lady Wilde realised the link between performing the Stations and pagan rituals of old. This is what she had to say about it:

Much of the ancient Druidic ceremonial has been preserved by the people, such as the symbolic dances, the traditions of sun-worship, and other pagan rites, which were incorporated into the Christian ritual of well-worship by the early converts, and are still retained, though [they] are now only practised as ancient customs, for which the Irish have great reverence, as having come down to them from their forefathers. The ceremonial is the same at all these places of devout pilgrimage. The pilgrims go round the well a certain number of times, either three or nine, creeping on their hands and knees, but always from east to west, following the apparent motion of the sun, and reciting paters and aves all the time. At the close of each round they build up a small pile of stones; for at the last day the angels will reckon these stones, and he who has said the most prayers will have the highest place in heaven, each saint keeping count for his own votaries. The patient then descends the broken steps to the well and, kneeling down, bathes his forehead and hands in the water, after which oblation the pain or disease he suffered from will be gradually removed, and depart from him for evermore.

Ancient Legends, Mystic Charms and Superstitions of Ireland

CLOG DUBH: HOW A WHITE
BELL TURNED BLACK

The famous Black Bell of St Patrick, or Clog Dubh, was a respected relic on Croagh Patrick for centuries. The story goes that the iron bell (which dates from AD 600–900 and was therefore made after Patrick's death) was originally white, but endured such a battering of demons while St Patrick was on the summit, that it became black.

The traditional stewards of the bell, the Geraghty family of Ballinrobe, used to take it up to the mountain on Reek Sunday. There, it could be kissed by penitents, or be passed three times around the body of those suffering ill health. In *A Frenchman's Walk through Ireland* (1797), De Latocnaye claims it was also 'used as a thing to swear on in legal matters, and no one will dare to perjure himself on it'.

Around 1840, Sir William Wilde (father of Oscar) bought the bell for the Royal Irish Academy from the Geraghty family, and it now resides in the National Museum in Dublin. Other names for it include 'Bearnan Bhrighde', the 'gapped bell of Brigid' due to its broken state, and 'Clog Geal' (Bright Bell).

The iron bell known as Clog Dubh

WORKING THE IRON AGE SYSTEM: THE SECRET OF SUCCESS

For Patrick's mission to have even a chance of succeeding, he had to schmooze as many of Ireland's VIPs as possible. From the Boyne Valley to the plains of Mayo to the loughs of the north, there were between eighty and two hundred *tuath*, or territories – and Patrick's method was the same in all of them. Upon entering a tuath, Patrick would approach the highest-status chieftain or king he could find and try to bring them onside. His inspirational preaching went some way towards his goals, but he also used traditional Brehon methods.

BREHON NETWORKING

There was a great tradition of hospitality among the Celtic elite. A chieftain's worth was measured by his ability to provide generously for his guests, his vassals and his allies. There was also a specific class of people known as brughaidh, or hospitallers, who were required to open their home and provide for any visitors. Sometimes they would receive so many visitors they would lose all their assets. Still today, the Irish are famous worldwide for their custom of hospitality.

So when Patrick came into an area, as a high-status bishop, he expected and usually received food and accommodation from the local chieftain. In return, Patrick gave gifts to the chieftains, such as cattle, horses and chariots.

Patrick also used another ancient Brehon custom – fosterage.

In this age-old system the sons and daughters of a family were sent to another family to be educated until they were around fourteen years old at which time they returned home. In this way the children returned having formed a strong bond with their foster family, and also having acquired new skills and accomplishments. This resulted in a complex network of alliances. In Patrick's version of fosterage, the sons of chieftains were offered the chance to travel with and be educated by high-status clerics. The legend says this is how he first met the child who later became St Benignus of Armagh, Ireland's first native bishop (see Inver Dé, page 141).

After a certain amount of this sort of diplomacy and if all went well, the chieftain granted Patrick land for a church and instructed his own tribal vassals to convert to Christianity. In many cases, the chieftains went on to become the local bishop (for example, St Sinach of Aghagower in County Mayo). In this way, the rich stayed rich and the poor stayed poor, and the hierarchies of centuries remained intact.

Sometimes, however, the reception wasn't so warm and there were occasionally pockets of resistance. Patrick says in *The Confessio* that he was taken hostage at least twice, though he doesn't go into details. One of the most famous stories took place at Tara, where Patrick experienced a fierce stand-off – and not just with any ordinary chieftain, but with Loegaire, the high king of Ireland himself.

THE FIRE AT SLANE

'I am to be buried in the earthworks of Tara, I, the son of
Niall of the Nine Hostages.'
Attributed to King Loegaire

The hills of Slane and Tara attracted the earliest cultures in Ireland. Myths tell us how Sláine, the king of the Fir Bolgs, was buried at Slane, giving the place its name. The hill also features in the famous story of the *Táin Bó Cuailnge*. Just to the south of Slane lies the Hill of Tara, from where one can see twenty-two counties on a good day. Occupied for more than 2,000 years, Celtic royalty was inaugurated at Tara; every third year, during the festival of Bealtaine, the king called a major assembly during which a sacred fire was lit.

By the time of Christianity's arrival in the early fifth century, the sacrifices of firstborn children, lambs and calves by fire had become symbolic. Children and animals were merely herded between two sacred fires, and not burnt in them. But the fire itself remained sacred to the earth mother Danu, and symbolised the springtime reawakening of the world, after the long sleep of winter.

PATRICK CHALLENGES THE HIGH KING

In the spring of AD 433 King Loegaire ordered his druids to light the fire on the hilltop of Tara, and prepared to preside over sacrifices to the gods, the proclaiming of the Brehon laws by his

Aerial view of the Hill of Tara, County Meath

bards, and the drinking and carousing by the assembled royal court and selected VIPs. By ancient custom, no one was allowed to light their bonfire before the king, on pain of death.

Suddenly a shout went up. Royals, druids, generals and governors all squinted northwards to the Hill of Slane where they saw a bonfire blazing brightly. It was Patrick, with his own beacon of light and nothing if not provocative, choosing to celebrate not the rebirth of the land, but the resurrection of Christ at Easter.

They had all heard of this man, this future international saint. The druids had been foretelling for years that 'a certain foreign practice' would kill all the kings in Ireland. Now he was here and had thrown down his challenge.

Aerial view of the Hill of Slane, County Meath

CONFRONTATION

The story goes that the furious druids proclaimed that the fire had to be put out that very night or it never would be. Loegaire wasted no time. He demanded the death of the man who had committed the sacrilege. Within minutes, the king, his two most senior druids and twenty-seven chariots were galloping across the plain of Meath, heading for the Hill of Slane.

When they arrived, Patrick walked toward the king, praying loudly. A pagan courtier named Erc immediately converted. (He was later appointed the first Bishop of Slane, and is believed to have ordained Brendan the Navigator, one of the Twelve Apostles of Ireland.)

The warriors rained insults on Patrick, who called on his God to deal with them. At that moment darkness descended. One of the druids fell over and fractured his skull on a stone. An earthquake overturned the chariots. Chaos reigned while Patrick prayed on. Finally, he and his disciples shape-shifted into deer and escaped into the wilds.

FEAST AT TARA

The next day, on the intercession of the queen, King Loegaire invited Patrick to the feast at Tara. But the wily pagan had no intention of giving in – his real intention was to get rid of Patrick permanently.

The feasting was in full swing as Patrick arrived with his supporters, including a boy that he had fostered, Benignus. Neither the king nor his court stood to greet Patrick – an obvious sign of disrespect designed to show he was not welcome. Undaunted Patrick accepted a drink. This is what the *Leabhar Breac* (Speckled Book) a medieval manuscript, says happened next:

> The wizard (druid) Lucat-Mael put a drop of poison into Patrick's goblet, and gave it into Patrick's hand. But Patrick blessed the goblet and inverted the vessel and the poison fell thereout, and not even a little of the ale fell, and Patrick afterwards drank the ale.

This miracle made another courtier named Dubhthach convert on the spot, much to Loegaire's disgust.

DRUIDS VS MISSIONARIES

A magical contest then ensued between Lucat-Mael and Patrick, culminating in a trial by fire. Patrick built a hut, half of which was made of seasoned dry faggots and the other half made of sappy green wood.

Patrick suggested his faithful companion, Benignus, disguised in a druid's clothes, should go into the dry wood, while Lucat-Mael, wearing Patrick's own tunic, should go into the damp green wood. The hut would then be set on fire leaving God to decide who would survive. The druid agreed, possibly thinking that the green wood would never catch fire. Benignus agreed, possibly thinking he was about to meet his Maker. They entered the hut, the door was locked and the hut set on fire.

As Patrick prayed, the fire passed through the dry wood as far as Benignus. It managed to burn the druid's tunic he was wearing, but left the boy untouched. As for the druid, the fire completely consumed him and the damp green wood around him, leaving only Patrick's tunic behind.

When Loegaire saw this loss of yet another supporter, he was finally humbled. He went to the meeting place at Tara proclaiming it was 'better to believe than to die'. Then he knelt before Patrick and converted, along with hundreds of his people.

The story ends with Patrick predicting that Loegaire would rule many more years, but no member of his family would ever again be High King of Tara.

There are various versions of this most popular story. This nineteenth-century blessing for the hearth refers to it:

I bank down this fire with the miraculous powers
that Patrick got.
May the angels pile it;
May no enemy pull it apart.

POETIC PREDICTION

Druids and soothsayers, never known for their optimism, had sensed that their way of life was coming to an end. This poem may have been contemporary with Patrick:

Adze head shall come,
With a crooked-headed staff
In his house with a hole in its head.
He will chant blasphemy from his table,
From the eastern [front] part of his house,
And all his household will answer him:
'So be it, so be it.'
When all this happens
Our kingdom, which is heathen, shall not stand.

Saint Patrick: Ireland's Patron Saint, George Otto Simms

The 'house with a hole in its head' may be a chasuble, a kind of priestly poncho still worn today at Mass. Chanting 'blasphemy from his table' refers to preaching from the altar, which is traditionally in the 'eastern part of his house' or church. The household answering 'So be it,' refers to the response 'Amen' made by a congregation.

Stone of Destiny, Hill of Tara

WHAT THEY LEFT BEHIND AT TARA

The Stone of Destiny was where the High Kings of Ireland, likely including Loegaire, were inaugurated. According to legend, the stone would screech loud enough to be heard all over Ireland when touched by the rightful king. Excavations at the Rath of the Synods have unearthed Roman artefacts dating from the first to third centuries. It is believed the Romans went no further in their exploration of Ireland.

The Iron Age hilltop enclosure features many prehistoric earthwork and stone features, including the Fort of the Kings, Cormac's House and the Banqueting Hall.

A nineteenth-century church on the hill, named for Patrick, is now used as a visitor centre. To the north is a feature known as the Mound of the Hostages. This refers to a common practice by chieftains of keeping their rivals hostage as surety against the actions of their vassals and this spot is where the exchange took place. Patrick is said to have been briefly imprisoned here and, although there is no proof of that, the 5,000-year-old mound is certainly old enough.

To the south of the Fort of the Kings lies Loegaire's Fort. The king who had so many dealings with Patrick is said to have been buried here – but despite being baptised he was not buried lying down like a Christian. Instead it is said he was buried in an upright position, with a sword in either hand, like the pagan king he was.

The Mound of the Hostages, Tara's oldest feature

PUSHING AT AN OPEN DOOR

The pope in Rome had decided Ireland needed to be converted to Christianity, and despite some of the resistance encountered by Patrick at Tara and elsewhere, the Irish took to the new spiritual belief system surprisingly easily, and there was little bloodshed over it. Here are some of the reasons for such a smooth transition.

- The pagan Irish revered knowledge, particularly as it was delivered by the spoken word. Their poets were high-status members of society, so people were used to paying attention to gifted storytellers – and Patrick was probably an inspirational speaker.
- Pagan people already believed in the Otherworld. The stories they told and the songs they sang were a way to understand unseen forces and of heaven and hell. When Patrick talked of casting out devils, they understood that he was talking about real devils; when he talked of heaven, they already believed in it.
- Theirs had always been a passionate and blood-shedding society, as shown in the Fianna cycle of myths. So the Irish understood the idea of sacrifice – blood sacrifice, particularly – and appreciated the significance of the Crucifixion.
- Patrick's Holy Trinity – three gods in one – was at the heart of his

The three-pointed trefoil of Celtic design expresses the idea of 'threeness' teaching. But for the Celts, the idea of 'threeness' was already special: they had their own female version, the goddess Macha, who was venerated as three goddesses in one.

• The structure of society was rigidly hierarchical anyway, so the upper classes of chieftains, druids and Brehons, were much inclined towards another hierarchy of bishops, monks, and clerics. Many chieftains became abbots of communities and acting bishops. Christian communities often started near – or inside – a royal rath.

• The Irish loved hero tales. Patrick came to be seen as something of a hero, not unlike Cú Chulainn, the northern Irish mythical figure, who sacrificed his life for his people. This veneration may explain why Patrick is occasionally described as a giant.

• The missionaries were often revered and thought to be able to perform miracles, like their pagan counterparts, the druids.

• The early church set major rituals around the same time of year as the pagan ones. For example, Christmas occurred at the same time as the winter solstice, and Easter superseded the spring fire festival of Bealtaine. Today interest in pagan festivals has resurfaced and they are widely celebrated.

At the same time, the coming of Christianity coincided with the advent of writing, and this helped spread the new religion by becoming an essential part of the cult of Patrick.

THE CULT OF PATRICK

In the seventh century, nearly two hundred years after Patrick died, his cult began to gain momentum. Religious communities really started to reflect on Palladius and the other fifth-century missionaries and they found that they were shadowy figures, remembered only in folklore. Patrick, on the other hand, was going from strength to strength, his reputation and early foundations flourishing.

The writings of Patrick, the *Confessio* and *Letter to Coroticus*, made him concrete in the minds of his devoted followers. Through his words, he continued to 'speak' directly; in fact he started the *Confessio* with the words 'Ego Patricius', which simply means 'I am Patrick'. This gave the church something to build on. The writings were copied and recopied faithfully by monks and distributed far and wide. They carried in them their

author's authentic voice and a strong message from Rome. Nothing could compete, until the other missionaries were either forgotten or melded into the Patrick story.

SCRIBBLING MONKS

Two scholarly seventh- and eighth-century biographers, Muirchú and Tírechán, wrote about Patrick's extraordinary

Patrick wrote his Confessio, beginning simply 'Ego Patricius', or 'I am Patrick'

A page from the *Book of Armagh*

life and are responsible for many of the legends that we still associate with him today. Muirchú gave us the story about Loegaire and the fires at Slane and Tara, and also the story of the chieftain Dichu. He described the miracle of Daire brought back from the brink of death and he named Patrick's slave master, Milucc. Tírechán, on the other hand, is more interested in Patrick's itinerary around the island of Ireland – partly because he wanted his readers to compare Patrick with the prophet Moses. He is responsible for the famous story of the Lenten fast on Croagh Patrick. They both endowed him with hero traits, such as extraordinary strength, and claimed that he personally knew many legendary figures such as Fionn mac Cumhaill. By the ninth century, their works had been included in the beautiful *Book of Armagh*, along with the *Confessio* and the *Book of the Angel*, in which Patrick converses with a kind of heavenly estate agent who insists that Armagh is the best place in Ireland to locate the head of the church.

ARMAGH'S PROPAGANDA

Armagh used its possession of Patrick's works to claim dominance over – and therefore taxes in – all churches in Ireland. It was backed up by muscle – a confederation of fierce tribes, which had come together in the seventh century to overthrow the famous Uí Néill clan of the region and create a new order.

Other communities in Kildare (with its links to Brigid), Clonmacnoise, Iona (Scotland), Clones and Devenish also vied to be head of the Irish church. But as Armagh persuaded more and more vulnerable churches to pledge allegiance and join its federation, none of these others centres could compete. Armagh's spin doctors won the PR battle, because Patrick's texts provided better propaganda than anywhere else.

Devenish Island ruins, Lough Erne, County Fermanagh

ST PATRICK'S CATHEDRALS, ARMAGH

After the Reformation of the sixteenth century, the reformed Protestant faith made its way from England to Ireland. The Protestant Church of Ireland inherited the saints of the older Catholic religion, hence Patrick is claimed and venerated by both traditions. Although Catholicism was the original Christian religion in Ireland, the Penal Laws allowed Protestantism to flourish.

The town of Armagh is both the Catholic and the Church of Ireland See – that is, the ecclesiastical head of both religious traditions in Ireland. Therefore it boasts not one but two St Patrick's cathedrals – one Catholic and one Protestant.

ST PATRICK'S CHURCH OF IRELAND CATHEDRAL, ARMAGH

According to Tírechán, the local chieftain, Daire, agreed to give Patrick land, but he wasn't too happy with Patrick's request for prime land, known as Drumsaillech (the Hill of Sallows). Instead Daire gave him an inferior site lower down, and Patrick duly moved in there with his followers.

One day, the chieftain's horse strayed onto Patrick's land to graze. It died soon afterwards and Patrick was blamed for cursing it. Furious, the chieftain vowed to kill Patrick – but no sooner were the words out of his mouth than he himself had an attack of colic and looked to be dying. The story goes that his wife begged Patrick to sprinkle holy water on him and the horse, after which

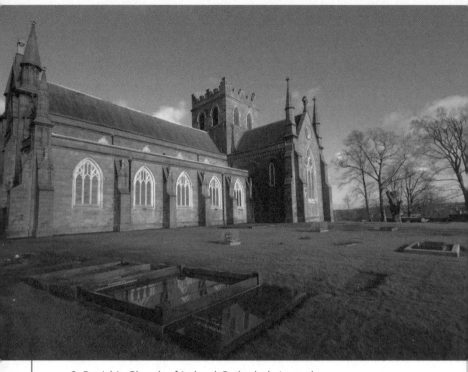

St Patrick's Church of Ireland Cathedral, Armagh

man and beast were both revived. The chastened Daire then offered Patrick the hilltop site he'd originally requested.

Around the year 445, Patrick built a great stone church at Armagh, which he decreed the premier church in Ireland. After several sackings and rebuildings, today's Church of Ireland cathedral stands on the same spot, still one of the largest churches in Ireland.

ST PATRICK'S ROMAN CATHOLIC CATHEDRAL, ARMAGH

The Catholic cathedral, on a hill nearby, was built much later than its Protestant counterpart, in the mid-nineteenth century after the repression of Catholicism was eased with the repeal of the Penal Laws in 1829.

According to the *Book of Armagh*, the cathedral site was chosen because, one day, Patrick went up to some high ground to look at the view. At the top he found a hind with her little fawn. His followers wanted to kill and eat the pair of them, but Patrick refused. He carried the fawn on his shoulders, with its mother following, and released them at a place called Tealach na Licci (Sandy Hill). Some 1400 years later the Catholic cathedral was built on the spot where Patrick released the fawn. In a niche at the front of the building there is a statue of Patrick holding his famous golden crozier. Inside there are many stained-glass depictions of the conversion of Irish pagans.

Saint Patrick's Roman Catholic Cathedral, Armagh

MURDEROUS MACHA

It is said that a goddess founded Armagh. Macha, a semi-historical pre-Christian tribal princess gave her name to the hill and surrounding area on which is built the city (Ard Mhacha meaning Height of Macha). The much older Eamhain Mhacha (Navan Fort) nearby was also named for her. It had been the royal seat of the kings of Ulster, until it was destroyed and over-taken by Armagh.

Another version of this female is Macha, the Irish goddess of war, who is closely linked to the land and to horses, and is seen as a slaughterer of men. One story about Macha tells how she attended the assembly of the king of Ulster. Her husband boasted that she could run faster than any horse and the king insisted that she demonstrate, despite the fact that she was heavily pregnant. She raced the king's finest stallions – and won, giving birth to twins on the finish line. But Macha cursed the men of Ulster, saying that they would suffer her labour pangs in the hour of their greatest need. And so it came to pass – it is the reason Cú Chulainn had to fight the armies of Connacht all alone in the legend of the Táin ('The Cattle Raid of Cooley').

Opposite: The remains of Navan Fort, County Armagh

PART TWO

PATRICK'S STORY

The rocky coast of Northern Ireland

The Year of Our Lord 402, Somewhere
along the West Coast of Britain

Birdsong woke me. I stretched my long limbs, leapt out of my bed and strolled outside. I sniffed the air; sea salt and the fragrance of spring were all around, but it was chilly enough and I could see my breath. I ran back inside for my new cloak. Mother laughed at me, because I was only going out to collect kindling with the other boys.

'Maewyn', shouted one of the boys through the door of our house. 'Don't get your fancy clothes dirty!'

I grinned and held my cloak out of the mud. It was better than most of the boys could afford. My father gave it to me when I reached fifteen summers last year, saying I was nearly a man. He was a generous person, especially when his livestock were fat and the Roman tribunes ordered a lot.

My father and his father before him had spent their lives doing business with the Roman garrison up the road, and he was used to a high standard of living. Not for Calpurn's family a hut, like our neighbours; we lived in a house made of stone. It wasn't as grand as a villa, of course, but it was a few steps up from mud and straw. And it was next to the chapel, which my father loved and looked after.

My father wanted me to follow in my grandfather's footsteps as a priest. It was a good job, he said, with plenty of money attached. But I wasn't interested. I could read and write of course – I had been taught well by the clerics my father employed – but I wasn't keen on a life of learning. I wanted to be outside, running things. I wanted to be doing things. My parents tried to make me attend the chapel too, but I wouldn't go. Father was disappointed in me, but the truth was I had always been stubborn. I enjoyed the old religion, like many of the folk around here, and all the stories about nature and animals and gods. Father said I wouldn't get anywhere in life, if I carried on like that.

It was turning into a beautiful sunny morning. I picked up a few sticks and gazed down over the bay. The sea was a brilliant blue and the white sand glistened. There were footprints all over the place, and I wondered idly who they belonged to. I watched the clouds scudding across the sky and tried to figure out what I would do with my life.

Things were changing fast around here, and not for the better, everyone said. There was no villa-building or road-building anymore, no tiling or stonework – the craftsmen were all gone elsewhere. There were hardly any soldiers around, so who was defending our patch of coastline, people kept asking.

I sometimes thought the unthinkable. What if the garrison were to get the word from Rome to pull out altogether? The soldiers could be packed up and gone in a matter of weeks – days even. They were ruthless like that. And as for us? We'd be left to our fate, and any barbarian with a boat could come and take anything they liked. Any barbarian with a boat …

I looked again at the footprints on the sand. And that's when I heard it. A shriek, slicing through the spring air. It was a signal. With an enormous crash, a group of men – twenty or thirty of them – suddenly came thundering out from the trees, yelling.

I dropped my sticks and ran. The raiders were from across the water, I could tell by their blue-patterned bodies and long hair. I knew what was happening – I had heard tell of it around the fire. They took the young, the fit, the healthy, and they stole them back to their own savage land, to be worked to death ...

Where were my brothers and sisters, my friends? Some had gone down near the shoreline. They would be done for. I kept running, pounding towards the village. My breath was catching and my side was stabbing but I kept going.

The alarm had gone up in the village and people were pouring out of the huts, ready to defend what was theirs. I was nearly there. I would grab my father's axe off the wall and defend my home.

I heard heavy footsteps thundering behind me. Suddenly a huge weight fell on me from behind and my face hit the dirt. Guttural words were shouted at me in a language I did not understand. I twisted and turned. I bit, I scratched, but the man was huge and would not let go. I yanked his hair as hard as I could and got a stinging slap across the face. I was dizzy for a second and then I felt myself being dragged, kicking, along the ground.

I opened my mouth and screamed.

I could see my parents racing up the hill, shouting, but three of the biggest raiders blocked them. Through my blood and tears I saw my mother hurling herself onto one of the men. But he drew the point of a long knife across her forearm until her blood was flowing too. She kept screaming my name, arms outstretched, but she could not get through. My father fell on his knees, humbling himself before them, and begging for my life. He clasped his hands, pleading, and made the sign of the cross over and over again.

I was slapped around the head and half-pulled, half-pushed away towards the woods and down towards the shore. All I could hear was my mother's voice on the wind, calling my name over and over.

'Maewyn! Maewyn!'

Then I was thrown into the bottom of a boat and a sheepskin thrown over me, and I saw and heard no more.

Capture by Irish slave traders

Across the Sea

When I opened my eyes again it was dark and I was freezing. I was lying next to two others in the bottom of a large, hide-covered boat. There were ropes binding my wrists that were linked to a thick one around my neck. My nostrils were filled with the smell of wool grease and blood. My own blood was spattered down my tunic.

There were two raiders rowing the boat, which skimmed along the choppy waters, and two more sitting at the bow. Seeing me awake, one of the raiders in the bow nudged his companion. I tried to stand – but the rope choked me back. The men laughed. After all, where would I be going? The salt spray stung my eyes as I scanned the horizon. There were at least ten other boats in the fleet. My homeland was nowhere to be seen.

There was a girl beside me and she was weeping and the young lad on the other side was trying hard not to. They spoke the same language as me, but they were not from my village. I comforted them as best I could, telling them that they should stick with me, that we would fight to escape as soon as we could. They just stared at me with red, frightened eyes and did not speak any more.

We headed into the setting sun as the evening wore on. The night was cold and windy and we huddled together for warmth. The raiders put up the sail. I grew very thirsty but when they offered me water I haughtily refused.

Hour upon bitter hour passed. In the dawn light, a green fuzz appeared on the horizon. I could see mountains and the smoke from houses spiralling upwards onto the morning air.

At last the fleet of boats turned into an inlet, which opened out to a wide blue loch. The raiders were looking alert now, sailing close to land and scanning the green shores of the loch. One of them downed oars and picked up a goatskin bottle. He tipped his head back for a drink and then poured water into the mouth of each of us in turn. This time I did not refuse. I gulped the brackish water, and I opened my mouth for more.

At last we came to a place where there were fires lit by the side of the loch. There were people standing in small groups, and cattle, pigs and sheep grazing nearby.

The Slave Market

The four raiders jumped into the shallows at the same time and pulled the boat to shore. One took hold of the rope that fastened us to the boat and hacked it off with an axe. He yanked the ropes to make us get out and we all stumbled up the beach.

Other boats moored near us, and other youths, mainly boys, were forced out of them. I knew some of them by name and others only by sight, but when I shouted over to them I was walloped around the head.

The raiders were laughing and greeting each other with slaps on the back. There were fires on the beach and goatskins of drink were passed around. A couple of sour-faced ones herded us into a roped-off enclosure by poking us in the backs with spears. They stood guard; we were not allowed to sit down. I planted my feet firmly on the ground and stretched my limbs as well as I was able.

By the time the sun had climbed to its height, more men and

women had assembled and the air was ringing with the sound of what I guessed to be bartering. They walked among us and looked us over and murmured with each other. One dark-haired man approached, taller than the rest and wearing a golden torc around his neck, a sign of his high status. He grabbed me by the chin and looked at my teeth. Then he asked me my age, haltingly in my own tongue.

I refused to answer him, and stared him straight in the eyes. A guard poked me hard in the shoulder with his spear. Still I refused to answer.

The dark man grabbed my upper arms and squeezed hard. He looked at me calculatingly, and turned to my guard. They walked off down the beach a little way and I saw them spit on their right hands and slap them together.

When they came back the dark-haired man was grinning. He undid my rope and pulled me up the beach to a spot where there was a two-wheeled cart harnessed to a pair of small ponies.

I knew it. I had known all along. This was Ireland, that savage land to the west, where even the Romans would not go. I had heard all about it from my father. It was a land where there were no towns, no villas or churches, no books. They worshipped an old religion here, warrior goddesses and dark idols; people said they ate their own young …

And now I was among them, trapped, bought and paid for.

Milucc's Homestead

We rode for hours through the forests in the cart. My new

master gave me some bread but spoke only once, jabbing at his own chest and saying his name, Milucc, Milucc. He did not ask me mine. As we travelled I could see through the trees several mysterious stone circles just like those I had seen at home, and also standing pillars, some with strange runes carved into them. Later I found out they were an early way of writing, but they were not like any writing I had ever known.

Eventually we came into open land again and seemed to be climbing. The day grew chilly and I pulled my cloak, now torn and stained with sea water, around me. A couple of times I must have nodded off to sleep but jerked awake again when the wheels hit holes in the trackway. It seemed to be all trackways in this country, plunging in and out of the forest and across the glistening bogs. Not once did I see a paved road.

Milucc skirted round a tall, curved ditch, and turned in through a gate that led into an enclosure. We passed three or four round, thatched houses until we got to a big one in the middle. We got down from the cart and he led me inside this house.

Milucc's home was quite small by our standards at home, but much bigger than the others, and it seemed full of people. About twenty stout posts held up the roof and sides of meat were hanging from the rafters. On one side were five beds, and beside them a massive weaving loom. Near the door were two long shelves made of hazel twigs; one held pots and knives, and the

Ogham stone

other held a long sword and a round iron shield decorated with red birds. In the middle of the building there was a large fire. A huge iron pot swung gently over it from which wafted aromatic steam in my direction. My stomach gurgled.

I was pushed down onto a pile of animal skins next to the wall and Milucc tied me to a post. He sat on a large stool away from me and a young woman came and washed his feet and gave him a plate of bread and meat. A man the same age as him stood before him and spoke loudly, seemingly in rhyme and to great applause. Milucc nodded all the while and smiled.

An older woman with a kind face brought me a bowl of porridge to eat and a cup of fresh milk to drink. I fell on the food, ravenous. The next time I looked up, a small boy and two girls from the other side of the room had sidled up to me, staring with big eyes at me, the stranger. I took no notice of them or anything else around me; warm and fed for the first time in two days, my head grew heavy and I fell asleep where I sat.

I woke at dawn to the feel of a chicken running across my body. For a confused moment I forgot where I was, but then I felt the rope collar around my neck and heard laughter and the chatter of the strange language and I remembered everything.

The door was wide open and children, chickens and dogs ran in and out as they pleased. As I peered through the door, I could see a grain store, another small building with animal skins hanging inside, and a fenced enclosure for pigs and cattle. There was a quernstone where women were already grinding oats. Beyond the high earthen wall surrounding the enclosure rolled brown and green fields hemmed in by green woods.

All that day and the next people came in and out of the hut to

Early Celtic homestead

look at the new slave. They left Milucc gifts, such as meat or a bag of barley. The children tried to talk to me but I could understand nothing, and all the while I remained tied up.

At night people gathered in the hut to talk, sing and tell stories. Milucc instructed the women to feed all-comers and give them drink also. It seemed the custom. His issued orders, his golden torc glinting in the firelight, and his men standing by his side, and I realised my master was a man of importance.

But I seemed to be his only slave. There were no slave quarters in the enclosure, like there were back at home, and there were no other slaves nearby in the other huts. It was the women and girls who did most of the chores.

As at home, the women spent the day tending the central fire box. They washed and spun the wool from the sheep carcasses that hung around the place. Outside they ground barley and oats and rye, cut firewood, fetched water from the river, and foraged for roots and berries and birds' eggs. They looked after the children and all the animals, except the cattle and horses.

I guessed that the children were too young to work much; it looked like Milucc needed to produce more food, and that was why he had bought a slave.

A New Home

One morning, once he was sure I wasn't going to die, Milucc untied me from the post but left my hands bound to my neck rope. The skin on my wrists and neck was red and sore by now, but I wanted to show I wasn't beaten. I scrambled to my feet and stretched as far as I could.

He pushed me outside. He pointed around the woods and fields, and jabbered in his own Irish language. I stared at him, and with an effort, he said in my language: 'You run away. You die.'

He made me take my cloak off and place it on the ground. He took a bundle of sheepskins from a hook and tied it to my back. He led me through the gate of the enclosure and through a small wood and up a winding, stony track. He had my rope in his hand the whole time.

The track wound on and on, out of the wood and up the side of a hill until eventually it gave out altogether. We carried on upwards through rocks and black turf. I looked around me; this was not like the hills and valleys of my home. The hills here stretched for miles and they were bare at the top, except for boulders and rough grass. Down the hillside there was green

89

unbroken forest. All around there were mountain sheep and lambs grazing on the hillside. They all had a blue mark on them.

We came to a stone hut with a rounded roof, built next to a small brown stream. The hut was too low for a man to stand in but long enough to lie down. It had a wooden door and the floor inside was bare earth.

Milucc untied the bundle from my back and threw it into the hut. He placed some bread on top of the bundle, and stood back. He spoke for a while in his own language, pointing at the pregnant ewes, and then he untied my hands.

And, with that, he left me on the mountain, as surely imprisoned as if I was covered in chains. I waited until he was out of sight before I knelt on the ground and wept into the hard, cold earth.

Life as a Slave

It was lambing season, and I had to tend the sheep and save as many lambs from freezing to death as possible. I was not allowed a fire, but I had the shelter and Milucc came once a day with food and to check his animals. He was always repeating instructions in his own language, and I realised it had similarities to my own, and I could understand some of what he said.

I spent my first few weeks on the hillside, looking for any other people, or any possibility of escape. But there was none – only miles and miles of woods and bogland stretching all around me, with no smoke or any other sign of a living human being. If I ran away into that, I knew I would soon get lost, and drown or starve.

At home we often had passed an evening by telling ghost stories around the fire, and I remembered every word of them now. Each night I cowered in fear at the howling of wolves and wild cats, and at the wicked spirits that I knew lurked outside my hut. I often lay sleepless until dawn.

My memories of home warmed me and tormented me. I dreamed of my parents, my friends, the fire in our house, the many comforts I had taken for granted. Now I was freezing, nearly naked and frightened. I worked all day minding the silly beasts on the hillside and had not enough to eat. Worse I had no one at all to talk to. I wept when I thought of playing games with my friends, carving shapes from wood, singing and telling jokes of an evening, and even reading quietly or practising my letters with the priest.

As spring turned to summer, the hillside buzzed with insects, and white hawthorn waved in the wind, but I was so lonely. When Milucc came, I smelled the woodsmoke on his clothes, and it made me long to go back to his hut. I begged him to bring me down to his people – just for a few days, just for one day! I promised I wouldn't try to run away – I needed to be with other humans, because I was beginning to forget that I was human myself.

One day he agreed. I followed him back down the hillside to the homestead, not to rest, but to work with the other men. The sheep would graze during the summer, and he needed me to look after the pigs and do repairs to his building and fences.

I slept in the pigs' enclosure but each evening I was allowed into the hut with the family. I felt the blaze of a fire for the first time in months. Because the children chattered to me every day, I now began to understand their language. The women warned them not to interrupt my work but I was glad of their company and their cheerfulness.

I hadn't realised before but there was more than one wife and mother here – Milucc seemed to have a main wife and a second wife, both of whom had children. They were up at dawn, working every day alongside me. Milucc, meanwhile, once he was sure I would not run away, spent most of his time outside with the other men, hunting and minding his cattle.

The Pagan Feast

The summer turned into autumn, and the days became shorter and colder. One night, a full moon shone down on the homestead turning it at light as day, and the people held a feast. People came from other homesteads, and one brought a slave with him. She looked about my age and she was pregnant. I felt so sorry for her, the poor girl had been ripped from her family as I had been from mine, and what would happen to her and her baby? We were kept apart and not allowed to speak to each other.

The people called this feast Samhain. It was a big celebration of the turning season. The adults had slaughtered a pig and cooked special food for the spirits of the Otherworld. Then Milucc commanded that all the fires be quenched in the homestead. They drank mead and competed in drunken games. The children crafted straw headdresses and ran around trying to scare each other.

Later all the people gathered in the main house. They spent

the darkest hours singing and telling thrilling stories of their gods and heroes, and the men reminisced about their own battles. Milucc's poet told how, every Samhain, a hero named Fionn mac Cumhaill saved the High King in Tara from a goblin who lulled his victims with sweet music, and then burned down the hill fort.

A wise woman told a story about how the tribe's forefathers used to sacrifice humans to the gods. When food was scarce, they would choose the highest-born, healthiest young man of the tribe, take him to a sacred place out in the bog, and kill him there, letting his life blood soak into the ground as a gift for the gods. I was frightened when I heard this but the people only laughed at my fears and made me understand they no longer sacrificed people and, anyway, I was too low in status to be chosen.

They made fun of my Roman manners. I retorted that we had old ways in my homeland too, and I knew as much about the old spirits as I knew about the One God of my father and grandfather. Then they brought me into the centre of them and made me sing a song from my homeland, giving me food and drink all the while.

Just before dawn, Milucc's druid came to him bearing a torch made of hazel twigs. He had built a sacred fire in the stones on the hillside where no one would go and now offered it as a gift to Milucc. Milucc relit his fire and, from the swirling smoke, the druid forecast he would gain many fat cattle in the year ahead. Milucc then gave out brands from his fire to the people. They staggered away to their own homes to light their own fires and sleep.

The First Winter

The day after the feast, Milucc forced me up the hillside again for the winter. I begged him to let me stay with the people but he was unmoved. He increased my food ration though. Maybe he felt sorry for me, or maybe he didn't want his most expensive possession – me – to die in its first year. Milucc said he could not spare any firewood for my hut, and warned me that if I lost any of his animals in the storms, he would beat me. Then he gave me an extra animal skin to make up for his harsh words.

I faced that first winter convinced that I would die. My fear, my hunger, my exposure and my loneliness became almost too much to bear. And worse than all of these were the feelings of powerlessness and shame I had about myself. Why had this happened to me? Could I have done anything to prevent it? Was I being punished because I had not obeyed my father and grandfather?

I remembered with shame the slaves in my own village, some owned by my father, and how they had been all but invisible to me. They too had had homes and families, but I had ignored them. Now my humiliation was the same as theirs.

Fasting and Praying

One night as I tried to sleep in my hut, I remembered how the pagans had feasted in the autumn and how pathetically grateful I had been to eat and drink with the rest, but how I had been put out again on the hillside. Suddenly, I knew I would never be one of them – I was different. I was a Briton. I was a Christian. And I was a slave. I would not survive if I did not find strength from somewhere.

Then it came to me, the words of a prayer my mother had taught me. I hadn't been interested at the time, but now it was as if I heard her voice inside my head, and I found I could recite it word for word. I did it once. I did it twice. I recited it a third time and felt better. The next morning I did the same, and the next morning after that. And the more I prayed, the better I felt.

After that, I said this prayer, and any others I could remember, every day and every night, over and over again. I felt closer to my family than I had at any time since my capture. I thought of them saying the same words hundreds of miles from me. And I thought deeply about the stories and the sacrifices of the One God, and I constantly begged for His help.

If I had known how long I would have to wait for my liberty, I think I would have lain down and died then and there. But luckily we cannot know what is in store for us, so I survived that wild winter and I survived five more like it.

I became a man while I was on those hills, strong and hardy. Every day I lived, I knew I was getting stronger – and I knew why. As the time went on, I prayed in ice, rain, wind and snow, and I got up at night to go outside and pray under the stars.

Milucc would laugh whenever he came and saw me doing it, but so long as it didn't interfere with my work he didn't care. Both his wives forbade me to do it in front of the children, but they, curious like all children, used to come and ask me about the One God when their parents weren't looking.

I never again celebrated a festival with the people as I had that one time, even though they always tried to make me join in. Instead, every winter when they held their shortest day festival of sacrifices and carousing, I celebrated Christmas alone in my hut with a night-long vigil. Every springtime when they held their fire festival, I celebrated Easter, the most important festival of all. I prayed special prayers and covered my hut with flowers.

I fasted often and was fierce if anyone mocked me.

The Voices

At some point I started hearing voices at night during prayer, soft, friendly voices from Heaven. They helped and supported me in my loneliness. But then in the sixth year of my bondage, I heard different voices in a dream. They were so vivid, so wonderful and so frightening, that I couldn't stop thinking about them. They sang to me that all would be well, and that I was destined for Heaven. I fasted and prayed even more, and the voices told me I did well and would stay strong.

And then, one night, the voices told me I was going home.

I implored them in my prayers: how was I to get home? I was the property of an important man, and as soon as I went missing from this mountain I would be rounded up, beaten and brought back. And that's if I wasn't devoured by wolves or bears, or fall in a bog, or die of exposure and starvation.

The voices continued. They were calm, reassuring. My ship was ready. It was two hundred miles away. I was to leave my master and walk to the coast. I would know what to do when I got there.

I knew only my hills, the homesteads and forts near here, and the rivers. I knew there were ancient trackways through the forest to the beach where I had landed six years earlier. But what if I got lost in the forest?

'Have faith,' said the voices.

They would help and guide me to the right place, far south of where I was. I listened and I trusted.

Over a week, I saved some nuts and bread and bilberries from my small ration. I wrapped them in a nettle cloth I had made, and hid it. I said goodbye to Milucc's children in my own language. They laughed at me, thinking I was joking with them.

Then one May evening, as the sun was setting, I faced south and started walking.

Escape

I walked for fourteen days and nights, always southeast, always through forest, and resting in caves whenever I could. My food lasted a few days and then I picked roots and fruits. In the woods there were wolves and vicious wild boar and, one night, I had to use just a branch to fight off a big wild cat. I was stung and bitten by flies. I quickly grew dirty and smelly, and my hair became matted.

When I came to villages I begged, and I'll say this for the people, they always gave me something. I have never known anything as generous as the ordinary Irish, from the lord to the cowherd. In one small homestead, as well as food, two girls made me sit down. They put a poultice on my bleeding feet, and tied them with clean rags. In another place, an old man gave me a tunic because mine was in rags.

One day I came upon a group of druids, standing in a circle around a huge oak tree. I hid behind a hawthorn bush in bloom so they couldn't see me. It was a druid school, and they were all chanting the old knowledge together under the eye of one old man. He suddenly whacked one of the younger druids on the back of the knees with a switch, and I got such a start I made the bush shake. I knew he would return me to Milucc if he caught me, so I crept away as silently as I could.

The Ship

On the fifteenth day I could smell the sea. I staggered down onto a stony beach, and flung myself down in some rushes. Beside me there was a freshwater river flowing out to sea, and many hide boats moored on it, large and small, just like the one that brought me to Ireland.

I knew I was in the right place. But the harbour was busy and bustling with animals and market stalls and people, and I did not know how to find passage away from Ireland. Eventually I approached the captain of a large ship. He took one scathing look at me and sent me away, shouting curses down on my head as I slunk away.

By now I was so tired and thin I had no fight left in me. I crawled under a sheltered cliff nearby and I prayed and prayed until sunset. Then I slept.

I was awoken by a toothless crewman shaking me by the shoulder.

'Odd-looking creature, you are. Come. You'll bring us luck.'

I followed him out and stood on the beach. The first rays of the sun were lightening the horizon and the tide was about to turn. The scowling captain – the same who had sent me away – now beckoned me aboard the boat. He demanded I show submission to him in the custom of the pagans. This meant grovelling and sucking at his nipple, as if I were a dependent little baby. Many times I had seen Milucc insist on the ceremony with his vassals. I shook my head. I was done with pagan ways once and for all, even if I had to spend the rest of my life on this beach. The captain spat and turned away. He shouted the order to his men to set sail.

I gripped the side of the rocking boat and stared at the green hills of Ireland, shrouded in mist. The bright sun glinted on the loughs, and the sea was sparkling all around me.

I had been six years a slave. I had lost my home and my family, but I had not lost my future. I knew that all my hardship had prepared me for something, something so precious, that it made up for everything.

I knelt and gave thanks. Then I turned my face back to Ireland and gazed at it until the mist took it from view.

Patrick begs for help from a ship's captain.

99

PART THREE

TALL TALES FROM THE FOUR PROVINCES

This statue of St. Patrick
(who founded a church here
early in his Christian Mission)
was unveiled and blessed by
The Very Reverend
Jackie Conroy P.P.
on the
15th August 2006.

It is the final phase of
Aghagower's Millennium
Celebrations.
It was from here that
St. Patrick and some members
of his household accompanied
by St Benan of Kilbannon
departed on Shrove Saturday
in the year 441 to spend
40 days of Lent on
Croaghan Aigle
(now Croagh Patrick)
from whence they returned
on Holy Saturday to
celebrate Easter with
Bishop Sinach in Aghagower.

Stories about Patrick are told all over Ireland. It is likely, that as an evangelising missionary, he travelled extensively. But it is also the case that, as his cult status grew, people invented links with Patrick to enhance the holiness of their own place. Patrick's biographers, Muirchú and Tírechán, gave us some idea of Patrick's itinerary as well as his methods, which were, generally, to arrive and preach, convert the local chief, found a community, and move on.

Muirchú and Tírechán's itineraries for Patrick differ wildly from one another but one thing they agree on is that he made first landfall on the east coast near Wicklow. According to Muirchú, after sailing to the east coast near Wicklow, Patrick sailed north towards Ulster, stopping at Inishpatrick. He said mass on what is now Slieve Patrick. He then went back south by boat along the coast, into the Boyne Valley at Drogheda, and travelled by chariot towards the west. Meanwhile, according to Tírechán, Patrick landed on the east coast and worked his way through Meath to Uisneach in Westmeath. He went west and crossed the Shannon via Swim Two Birds. He went through Roscommon, Sligo and northwest to Mayo. It was then that he went up Croagh Patrick and after that into northern Mayo, back over to Sligo, blessing the River Drowes along the way. He visited Donegal, Antrim and all of the northeast. He headed south again through Kildare and Carlow to the Rock at Cashel.

Most of the Patrick stories come from Ulster, which has more concrete evidence of his work than anywhere else.

NORTHERN LIGHT: STORIES FROM ULSTER

The stunning and varied landscape of Ireland has no match anywhere, and the eastern part of Northern Ireland is not only beautiful, but boasts the main wealth of sites associated with Patrick. Tourism Northern Ireland sponsors driving tours, walking tours and pilgrimages all over 'Patrick Country', as it is often known, taking in woods, springs, hillforts, islands, cities and cathedrals. The 132-kilometre (82-mile) St Patrick's Way Pilgrim Walk begins at the Navan Centre, outside the city of Armagh, and winds through rich countryside and historic towns to end at Down Cathedral in Downpatrick, where Patrick is said to be buried. It is signposted and takes six to ten days. Another route of similar length, St Patrick's Trail, is suitable for cars, and takes in Patrick-related and other ancient features from Armagh to Newry to Downpatrick, before heading north along stunning Strangford Lough to Bangor. There's an interpretative centre devoted entirely to Patrick in Downpatrick, with films, interactive activities for children, and accessible wall displays about the main sights to be seen around the region.

SLEMISH MOUNTAIN, COUNTY ANTRIM

According to Muirchú, when Patrick landed in Ireland, the first thing he wanted to do was return to the place of his enslavement more than twenty years earlier. He got back in his boat and headed up the coast towards the 438-metre (1,437-foot) mountain of Slemish, near Ballymena in County Antrim. He was

St Patrick's Trail, Slemish Mountain, County Antrim

looking for the hillfort of his old slave master, Milucc, whom he may have wished to forgive. He may have wanted to convert him too. Muirchú says he took gold with him because he knew Milucc was covetous of gold. According to Eoin MacNeill, an expert on early Irish law as well as chief of staff of the Irish Volunteers in 1916, Patrick simply wanted to buy his freedom, since he was, technically, still a slave in Ireland.

But whatever the motive, things did not go according to plan. When the old man heard Patrick was coming, he barricaded himself and all his possessions in his hillfort. He then set the whole place on fire, preferring to burn to death than bend the knee to his one-time slave.

According to a 1,000-year-old poem in Old Irish by the poet-saint, Fiacc, an angel named Victor appeared to Patrick in a dream and told him to go to Slemish as a free man:

Victor (the angel) said to the servant
Of Milcho: depart over the waves,
He (Victor) placed his foot upon a stone
His marks after him remained.

This 'trace' refers to natural indentations in the rock on Slemish and the neighbouring hill of Skerry. (Skerry is a transliteration of Sciridh Phádraig, meaning 'Patrick's rocky hill'.) One story relates how they are the marks of Patrick's own footprints when he stepped onto Slemish, searching for his old master.

THE BARN AT SAUL, COUNTY DOWN

When Patrick first returned to Ulster, his ship arrived at Strangford Lough, near what is now the town of Saul in County Down.

The legend goes that Patrick and his companions met with a swineherd, who took them to his master, Dichu, a local chieftain. The servant and master were Patrick's first converts in Ireland, and Dichu gave the missionary a nearby barn to say Mass in. The Irish word for barn is *sabhall*, and that is how the town of Saul, the site of Patrick's first church, got its name.

Visitors today encounter not a barn, but a stone-built church and round tower built in 1932 to mark the 1,500th anniversary of Patrick's arrival. Saul was the earliest cult centre for Patrick, before it was overshadowed by Downpatrick, where Patrick's presumed grave is located.

St Patrick's Memorial Church at Saul, rebuilt on the site of Patrick's first church in Ireland

PATRICK'S HUNGER STRIKE

We may think the practice of hunger striking dates from the twentieth century, when it was employed by Irish and Indian nationalists and British suffragettes – but it was happening in Ireland long before that. According to ancient Irish Brehon laws, it was a traditional method of protest used by lower-status persons against those of a higher status. One story relates how Patrick picked up on this Irish form of restorative justice-seeking.

He was travelling through a wood when he saw enslaved men trying to chop down trees with blunt, unsuitable tools. Their hands were bloody and they were getting nowhere. When he enquired, he was told that Dichu's brother, Trian, was forcing this unusual labour on his slaves as a punishment. Patrick went to Trian's house and 'fasted on him', that is, he stayed on the property, refusing all food and drink. The idea of having a guest in his home who might starve himself to death was so contrary to traditional Irish views about hospitality, that the ashamed Trian lifted the slaves' punishment.

DOWNPATRICK, COUNTY DOWN

In Down, three saints one grave do fill,
Patrick, Brigid and Columcille.
Traditional Irish rhyme

Downpatrick is one of the key sites associated with Patrick. He is thought to have died in nearby Saul in the 460s, when he was in his seventies (or alternatively in Glastonbury, England, at the rather less likely age of 120). The biographer Tírechán says that after his death, untamed oxen carried the body of Patrick as far as they could. They finally halted and buried him at Dún Lethglaise, the former stronghold of the Celtic god Leglish. The 'Dún', meaning fort or stronghold, was then renamed Dún Pádraig after its famous occupant, and this

The reputed grave of Patrick, Down Cathedral, Downpatrick,
County Down

name, over time, became Downpatrick.

Down Cathedral, a Church of Ireland cathedral on the Hill
of Down, is the place where Patrick's remains are said to be
buried. It had been an important centre of his cult from the
sixth century but went into decline when Vikings ravaged the
earliest churches and monasteries on this site in the eighth
and ninth centuries, and carried off everything of value. From
the twelfth century it was home to Benedictine monks but the
community was again destroyed after the Dissolution of the
Monasteries in the 1530s. Today the same spot is occupied by
an early nineteenth-century church, which contains statues and
stained glass telling Patrick's story.

The saint's grave is marked by a simple granite slab displaying
the name 'Patric'. The popular rhyme above claims that Brigid

and, later, Columcille, Ireland's other two patron saints, are buried alongside him.

RAHOLP, COUNTY DOWN

St Tassach of Raholp was with Patrick when he died, according to the biographer Muirchú. Tassach was a skilled artisan, making crosses and chalices. He is said to have made a famous relic, a revered jewelled crozier known as the Bachal Isu, which tradition says was given by Jesus to a hermit who then gave it to Patrick. It survived nearly a thousand years until the Reformation in the 1530s when it was publicly burned outside Christ Church Cathedral in Dublin. The ruins of a pre-Norman church, known as St Tassach's, survive in Raholp.

STRUELL WELLS, COUNTY DOWN

Between Downpatrick and Saul lies a beautiful valley with a collection of wells that gave the area its Irish name, Toibreacha an tSruthail (*sruth* meaning stream). It is one of the most significant of the holy water sources connected with Patrick.

One day, as Patrick was washing in a cold, clear fountain at Struell, he was heard to sing his way through the psalms of morning office – possibly to distract from the freezing water. From that moment on, the water gained miraculous healing powers, and Struell Wells grew into an internationally famous place of pilgrimage.

It was particularly popular around midsummer, when the waters were said to rise up and heal. But the date itself has

St Patrick's Well, Struell Wells, County Down

another significance. John the Baptist was said to be six months older than Jesus, so the church dated his birthday to 24 June – six months back from Christmas Eve. Handily, this took in the pagan summer solstice festivities too, making St John's Day one of the biggest feasts of the year. Now on midsummer nights, St John's Day fires burn all over Europe, from Scandinavia to Spain, Christian rites echoing pagan roots. Pilgrimages to Struell ceased in the eighteenth century because of Penal Laws against Catholics, Presbyterians and Quakers.

Today there are four seventeenth-century huts housing the wells. They are all supplied by the same stream directed through culverts underground. Pilgrims used the Drinking Well and the Eye Well for drinking water and bathing the feet or face, while in the Men's Well and Women's Well, they could immerse other limbs or even their whole bodies in the freezing, pitch-black water.

SLIEVE PATRICK STATUE, COUNTY DOWN

Overlooking Saul and Raholp there is a hill known as Slieve Patrick, formerly Slieve William, after the conquering King Billy of England (1650–1702). It acquired its current name when a huge statue of Patrick was erected on top to commemorate the 1,500th anniversary of the missionary's arrival in Ireland. Lit up at night, it can be seen for miles around.

At the top of the hill there are fantastic views – as far as Scotland and the Isle of Man on a (very) clear day. The devout can do a pilgrimage to the statue every June and take in fourteen Stations on the way.

ST PATRICK'S CHAIR AND WELL, ALTADAVEN, COUNTY TYRONE

Not far from Downpatrick and near to the beautiful Ulster Way lies Altadaven Glen. From the shadows of the trees and moss-covered boulders looms St Patrick's Chair, a huge two-metre-high stone block, sculpted by nature, which looks like a massive throne.

One translation of the name Altadaven is 'Demons' Cliff'. In pre-Christian times it was the site of druidic fertility worship, involving the pagan earth goddess Brigid and the late-summer festival of Lughnasa. Patrick heard of these activities while he was preaching in the nearby settlement of Clogher, and tradition has it that he stormed up to Altadaven and found devils there, which he drove over the cliffs, giving the area its name.

Beneath the Chair is St Patrick's Well. This is not a spring but

St Patrick's Chair and Well, County Tyrone

a bullaun (see page 38), which cures warts – and is said never to dry up. It is clear that this area is still a special place of worship; between the Chair and the Well, there are two rag trees where offerings continue to be tied.

HOLYWELL, BELCOO, COUNTY FERMANAGH

Now in the environs of the larger town of Belcoo, Holywell has been a site of pilgrimage for many centuries, and local people still perform penitential Stations here. If you look carefully at this spring – the water, which is said to be the coldest in Ireland, flows in two directions. According to the sign erected nearby:

St Patrick's holy well at Holywell, Belcoo, County Fermanagh

This sacred well was a Lughnasa site (an ancient harvest festival). Past generations held that Saint Patrick came here and Christianised it. The Stations are made from the last Sunday in July to 15th August, they are traditionally performed in bare feet … The estimated yield of water is 600 gallons per minute. Cures are said to be wrought for nervous disorders and stomach ailments.

A legend around here says that the site was once the home of Crom Dubh, once again banished by Patrick and his mighty crozier.

River Bann, Coleraine

COLERAINE, COUNTY DERRY-LONDONDERRY

The town and district was given its name by Patrick, when he passed through around AD 450. Popular tradition has it that the saint was given land by a local chieftain on which to build and the land was covered with ferns. So Patrick called it Cúil Rathain (meaning ferny corner). Some argue a more accurate translation is 'the rath, or fort, at the bend of the waters', the waters being the River Bann, which was blessed by Patrick as he crossed and recrossed it many times.

The local belief is that Patrick's monastery was burned down in the 730s, but was in the same location as the present day St Patrick's Church.

GRIANÁN OF AILEACH, COUNTY DONEGAL

On Greenan Hill, at the narrow neck of the Inishowen peninsula, looms the Grianán of Aileach, one of Ireland's most impressive ring forts. This ancient site was regarded as so significant in the second century that it was included in Ptolemy of Alexandria's map of the world. An earthen fort existed many centuries even before then, as far back as the Bronze Age.

The name 'Grianán of Aileach' can be translated as 'palace or temple of the sun', the Irish word grian meaning 'sun', and the popular Irish name Gráinne being the name of the sun goddess herself. It is likely that pagan sun ceremonies took place here at the significant turns of the year, the equinoxes of spring and autumn, and the solstices of summer and winter. Offerings were made and the sacred fire was lit in the fort on the hill, visible for miles around.

For centuries, the Grianán was the traditional seat of the O'Neills, once the most warlike and important clan in Ulster. But it is also associated with a number of ancient legends, particularly to do with the Dagda, the 'good god' in Celtic myth, who fought a battle against the supernatural race of Fomorians. The fifteenth-century *Book of Lecan* tells how the Grianán was built to protect the grave of the Dagda's murdered son, Aedh.

And there are more tales: that it is where the sun goddess Gráinne hibernates in winter; that Nuada of the Silver Hand, the first king of the the Tuatha Dé (also known later as Tuatha Dé Danann), is buried here and that under the fort lie the sleeping warriors of the ancient O'Neill, waiting only for a call to arms to awake ...

Little wonder then that in AD 450 Patrick made a beeline for the place. At the holy well, in front of the assembled clans people and neighbouring tribes, Patrick baptised chieftain Eoghan O'Neill, an important character and descendent of Niall of the Nine Hostages. Eoghan gave his name to Inishowen. This very public move away from the old to the new religion at this symbolic place of royal power sent a clear message to the whole peninsula. Of course, this is why Patrick chose it.

Today visitors encounter a restored nineteenth-century version of the fort. There are the remains of a stone circle, an empty prehistoric burial mound, and an ancient holy well. Several objects have been found there, likely to have been pagan offerings to the Otherworld, including a sundial, coins, and a gaming board.

Grianán of Aileach, County Donegal

INISHOWEN, COUNTY DONEGAL

The stunning peninsula of Inishowen has sites of prehistoric and early Christian activity. One local theory about the village of Clonmany (Cluain Maine) is that it was named for a deacon of Patrick's. The ruins of a seventeenth-century Church of Ireland church are on the same site as the early monastery.

According to local folklore, when Patrick visited nearby Carndonagh, he promised to build a church there if he had a good night's sleep. He must have slept soundly because the church he built gave the town its name Carn Domhnach (the burial place of the church).

ST PATRICK'S PURGATORY, LOUGH DERG, COUNTY DONEGAL

O lone son of Calpurn – since I name him –
O Virgin Mary, how sad is my lot! –
He was never seen as long as he was in this life
Without the track of tears from his eyes …

> From *At St Patrick's Purgatory*,
> by Donnchadh Mór Ó Dálaigh, thirteenth century

In some ancient legends, the Irish would not accept Patrick's teachings unless he was able to demonstrate that he could enter Purgatory and return. There is a story that one day, Patrick came to an island in Lough Derg (red lake). God appeared in a vision, led him into a wilderness, and pointed out a pit or cave that was the entry to Purgatory. He told Patrick that anyone who stayed a day and a night in Purgatory would be cleansed of all his sins. Patrick, of course, achieved this feat, and built his church over the site.

The precise location of Patrick's Purgatory is unclear because there are two islands in Lough Derg: Station Island and Saints Island, both of which were sacred pagan places. In legend, the location of the entry seems to have been a cave on Saints Island, which has since been demolished. Early monastic communities grew up on both islands.

One tradition tells of a knight named Owen that came to Lough Derg. He was taken by demons to witness poor souls being punctured, frozen, boiled, squashed, and nailed to wheels. He himself made it to Heaven – and centuries later the story inspired *Inferno*, the first part of Dante Alighieri's fourteenth-century epic poem *The Divine Comedy*.

It was in the twelfth century that Patrick's Purgatory became a destination of pilgrimage, with early penitents fasting for up to fifteen days in the cave at Station Island. They modelled themselves on Patrick, who:

> ... felt not the cold of the season;
> He stayed the night in the waters,
> With heaven to be blessed as his kingdom,
> He preached through the day on the hills.
>
> *Fiacc's Hymn*

In the seventeenth century, pilgrims were expected to fast for nine days. They were shut up in a dark hole for one of the days, and they prayed kneeling on small stones for the rest.

While the penitential aspect of many Christian pilgrimages has moved over time toward an easier and more joyful experience, serious self-deprivation and penitence continue at Lough Derg to this day.

The church here was destroyed and rebuilt several times, but the present huge church was built in 1931. Pilgrimage season begins in late May or early June and ends in mid-August. The pilgrimage is a three-day event open to people of all religions, or none, who must be at least fifteen years old, in good health and able to walk and kneel unaided. Few home comforts are allowed on the island – even rugs are banned!

Pilgrims fast from the previous midnight, then make the brief trip by boat to Station Island. Once there, they remove shoes and socks, and begin a cycle of prayer and liturgies at rocky Stations around the island.

Stations are quite elaborate at Lough Derg. There are a number of stops, including St Patrick's Basilica, St Patrick's Cross and St Patrick's Bed. Other popular saints get a location and name check along the way, including Brigid, Catherine, Brendan and Columba. As is usual, there are repetitions of Our Fathers, Hail Marys and Creeds, and circular walks around the Stations.

At some Stations the prayers must be said aloud, but at others silently. The prayers and the processions are mostly grouped in threes or multiples of threes – a strong link to the pagan veneration of the number three. When completing a Station, one always turns to the right.

Each day pilgrims eat one simple meal of dry toast, oatcakes and black tea or coffee, and they are not allowed to sleep until the second night. This vigil – or sleep deprivation for twenty-four hours – is the chief penitential exercise of the pilgrimage. If anyone is seen to be falling asleep, fellow pilgrims must wake them.

On the third morning pilgrims are ferried back to the mainland, where they continue their fast until midnight, but at least, at this point, tucked up in their beds, if they so wish.

KILLYCLUGGIN, COUNTY CAVAN

This townland of Coill an Chlogáin (wood of the little bell) was the home of the bell-shaped Killycluggin stone, also known as Crom Cruaich's stone. This is now in Cavan County Museum in Ballyjamesduff, and a replica resides on the stone's original site. The Iron Age stone had been placed near an earlier Bronze Age stone circle, which was an important place of pagan worship. Some say it was covered in gold, and people came from far and wide to worship the harvest god Crom Cruaich there.

Patrick reserved special fury for this gold-covered idol as it was known to be the focus of the most unspeakable kind of human sacrifice – children. According to a ninth-century collection of writings about Patrick, the *Tripartite Life*, Patrick whacked the idol with his golden crozier, and the idol broke into pieces. The rest of the stone circle sank into the ground with only the tops showing. Patrick lost the precious brooch fastening his cloak, and after the fight was won, he insisted that the grass of the whole plain be scythed short until the brooch was found.

Today the beautiful decorations on the replica Killycluggin stone can be seen clearly. The original, archaeologists say, does indeed bear the marks of repeated heavy blows on it.

ENDS OF THE EARTH:
STORIES FROM CONNACHT

Patrick's vision had been quite clear: he was to go 'hunting and fishing' for souls, and he was to go to the ends of the earth to do it. At a time when Jerusalem was seen as the centre of the world, and America was unknown, the 'end of the earth' was, literally, the west of Ireland.

Mayo was special to Patrick. According to Tírechán (who is possibly biased – he was a Mayo man, after all), the tradition that his slavery was served in Antrim appeared only after his death.

There are many place names and legends that commemorate Patrick in the west of Ireland, including holy wells and the ruins of early churches. Best of all, there is the Holy Mountain, and to it an ancient pilgrimage trail through beautiful, fierce countryside, known as the Tóchar Phádraig.

THE TÓCHAR PHÁDRAIG, COUNTY MAYO

St Patrick's Causeway, as nobody ever calls the Tóchar Phádraig, is a pilgrimage route going from east to west down ancient laneways and through the fields towards the Holy Mountain, Croagh Patrick. There had been a chariot road built around AD 350 that went from Rathcroghan (Ráth Cruachan), the seat of the rulers of Connacht, to Aghagower and onto Cruachán Aigle, as Croagh Patrick was then known.

After the coming of Christianity, pilgrims began to use this road as penance and to re-enact Patrick's ordeal. This continued for more than a thousand years until the reign of Elizabeth I and the Tudor reconquest of Ireland. As part of her draconian measures against the Irish of the west, there was a clamp down on travel, and the Tóchar fell into disuse. However, in the nineteenth century locals began to use it again, and by 1987 it was officially reinstated as a pilgrimage.

Today the Tóchar is thriving, the frequent rain and occasionally difficult terrain no deterrent to either religious pilgrims or keen hikers. Several organisations run tours in May, June, July and August, and there are alternative starting points – usually either at Ballintubber Abbey or 15 kilometres (9 miles) further east in the village of Balla, where Patrick used a holy well for baptisms. When starting from Ballintubber, the first day usually finishes at the once-important medieval settlement of Aghagower. The finishing point on the second day is, obviously, the mountaintop. For less hardy souls, it's advisable to stop at the village of Murrisk. When starting from Ballintubber, the Tóchar Phádraig is 35 kilometres (22 miles) long.

BALLINTUBBER ABBEY, COUNTY MAYO

Known as 'the church that refused to die', the abbey was founded in 1216 by the then King of Connacht, Cathal O'Connor, and underwent dramatic rises and falls in fortune, burnings, sackings and rebuildings. However, it is unique in that in all of its eight-hundred-year history, it is the only church in Ireland where Mass has been offered without a break, even throughout Penal times. The whole area takes its name from the well, Baile Tobair Phádraig, which Patrick used for baptisms in 441, and which can still be seen in a field at the back of the abbey.

The grounds of Ballintubber are packed with Patrick- and pilgrimage-related features of interest. The medieval remains of the pilgrims' hostel feature a ritual bath, or *dancora* (the word derives from *dabhach an chora*, or the 'bath of the righteous'), which is a wide, deep bath made of stone. Here pilgrims ritually washed their feet before setting off for Croagh Patrick, and, later, upon their return. Traditionally the water was heated by dropping hot stones into it. (In the fifth century, meat was cooked by the same hot-stone method in special cooking baths known as *fulachtaí fiadh*). There are other dancora remains in Balla and in Aghagower.

Ballintubber Abbey, founded in 1216

Early medieval ritual bath, Ballintubber Abbey

A statue of Patrick, unveiled as part of the abbey's celebrations in 2006, declares:

> Patrick and some members of his household accompanied by St Benan of Kilbannon departed on Shrove Saturday in the year 441 to spend the 40 days of Lent on Cruaghan Aigle (now Croagh Patrick), from whence they returned on Holy Saturday to celebrate Easter with Bishop Sinach in Aghagower.

In the grounds there are replicas of wooden churches of the fifth century. These *dairteachs* would have served as places of reflection or prayer, while baptism and the Eucharist were celebrated outside.

In a lush green field behind the abbey is the very spring that Patrick used for baptisms. Today it is clearly labelled with name and date, and decorated by an evocative sculpture of the saint bending over it, ready to go to work collecting souls.

BALLA, COUNTY MAYO

Medieval pilgrims along the Tóchar Phádraig used Balla as a place to gather and rest, and a monastery was founded in the

Statue of Patrick, Ballintubber Abbey

The natural spring behind Ballintubber Abbey, where Patrick performed many baptisms in 441

eighth century. Behind a beautiful round tower are the remains of a tiny hostel that has been restored in the original style of a house of rest, and, not one, but two sacred wells. One has fresh water still flowing and is accessible by rusty steps; the other is decorated with a statue of the Virgin.

AGHAGOWER, COUNTY MAYO

This historic village, with its ruined medieval church and tenth-century round tower, is a major stop on the Tóchar. Aghagower (Achadh Fobhair, meaning field of the springs) was a place of importance as an episcopal see (that is, a bishop's headquarters) until the 1200s and boasts some excellent maps and signs. One, incised in a marble slab, tells the visitor how to perform the Stations here.

Begin at the green enclosure, an avenue lined with trees, opposite the church. This leads to the Well of the Deacons (Tobar na nDeochán). The devout must go through the enclosure, praying a Pater (also known as Our Father), Ave, Gloria and a Credo followed by seven each of Paters, Aves and Glorias. Leaving the enclosure, the pilgrim must then walk seven times around the outside, saying any personal prayers they wish. There are two other Stations nearby, which are completed in the same way.

The Well of the Deacons and the Bath of Patrick (Dabhach Phádraig) were two natural springs, used for centuries for ritual purposes, but which dried up in modern times due to changes in local drainage.

A specially built enclosure for pilgrims to complete Stations, Aghagower, County Mayo

Well of the Deacons, Aghagower

In the ruined church's graveyard are the remains of Patrick's Bed (Leaba Phádraig), a small stepped plinth with a tiny altar on it. Though used by Patrick, this was not actually his sleeping place, as its sign makes clear:

Patrick's bed (Leaba Phadraig)
This enclosed area marks the first daytime shelter used by Patrick on his stay at Aghagower. It would also have been a temporary place of prayer until his workmen had built a church. It would not be used at night as the Chieftain Sinach would have provided nightly accommodation.

Pilgrims performed Stations between the bed and the Well of the Deacons, which has now dried up. Sinach was consecrated a bishop and received into the church by St Patrick. Sinach was the first bishop of Aghagower.

This St Sinach, the founder of the first community here, is a good example of the way Irish society maintained its class system from pagan to Christian times: Sinach was first a chieftain, and then a bishop, retaining his high status.

Round tower and Patrick's bed, Aghagower

MURRISK, COUNTY MAYO

The *Book of Armagh* has this to say about the village nestling at the bottom of Croagh Patrick:

> At Muiresc Aigli [Murrisk], Patrick buried his charioteer Totmáel, and gathered stones for his burial place and said, 'Let him be like this forever and I will visit him on the last days ...'

The village serves the Holy Mountain's many visitors. The root of the village's name is uncertain, but may come either from *muir riasc*, which translates as 'marsh by the sea', or possibly *Muir Iasc*, a sea monster worshipped in pagan times. Here, there is a Pattern Day on one Sunday a year.

According to Lady Wilde, nearby there is a lake called Clonvencagh (lake of revenge). People wishing ill would select a boulder or stone, stand it on end and support it with sand around its base, and perform rituals over it. This custom, with its roots in druidic ritual, gave rise to a local saying: 'he has been cursed by the stones'.

DID YOU KNOW?

The old custom among farmers is to turn the first sod of spring on St Patrick's Day.

WHAT IS A PATTERN DAY?

Traditionally, villages in Ireland celebrated their patron saint (*pátrún*) once a year on their feast day. Up until Penal Times this was done in churches, but after the destruction of many churches, the people went elsewhere – particularly to the local holy well. The devout walked and prayed around the well a set number of times, usually seven (see Stations, page 53). They might also drink the water and leave a token of their devotions, such as a pebble or a rag tied to a tree. Over time, these occasions became festive as well as prayerful, with singing, dancing and general craic an accepted part. Until, that is, such shenanigans were quashed by the clergy.

BOHEH STONE, COUNTY MAYO

East of Croagh Patrick and west of Aghagower lies the townland of Lankill and the Boheh Stone. The stone is set in a large outcrop of rock known as St Patrick's Chair, which is lavishly carved with circular cup-and-ring decorations, dating from the late Stone Age (4000–2500 BC). Some of these are similar to those found in the Boyne Valley, County Meath, showing how the culture of Neolithic people had spread right across Ireland. On specific dates, here you will experience the phenomenon known as the 'rolling sun'.

In 1987 a local historian named Gerry Bracken stood at the stone and looked west. He noticed a remarkable effect: the evening sun appeared to 'touch' the conical peak of Croagh Patrick, and 'roll down' down the north side of the peak as it set. From the Boheh Stone this phenomenon is visible on 18 April and 24 August and lasts twenty minutes. It is thought the stone was built here by sun worshippers who venerated this effect and connected it with the sowing and harvesting seasons. Today it is possible to book a guided walk to the stone on those dates.

BALLINA, COUNTY MAYO

After he crossed the River Moy Patrick came to the place that is now Ballina. This was the scene of many miracles, including healing a blind man and a lame man. On the Killala Road, there is a splendid modern shrine dedicated to Patrick. The shrine features a well, an altar, and Stations, and is decorated

Shrine dedicated to Patrick on the road to Ballina, County Mayo

with carved images of Patrick. The Irish inscription reads: *Is ag an áit seo a baistigheadh echaid mac nait ag naomh pádraic*, which means, 'This is the place where Eochaid Mac Nait was baptised by Saint Patrick'.

At Leigue Cemetery in Ballina, find a local to tell you the way to an ancient Bronze Age stone. Up a rocky path and now lying on its side, it has a circle-and-cross motif carving, which it is said to have been made by Patrick. (Some claim that the instantly recognisable Celtic cross itself was invented by Patrick, combining the sun of pagan worship with the cross of Christ.) Elsewhere in the grounds, the ancient Kilmoremoy Church was built on the ruins of Patrick's original church.

ST PATRICK'S CATHEDRAL, KILLALA, COUNTY MAYO

This nineteenth-century building is on the site of much older foundations. Samuel Lewis, in *Topographical Dictionary*, claims:

> … the Episcopal See of Killala appears to have been founded between the years 434 and 441, by St Patrick, who, during that period, was propagating the faith of Christianity in the province of Connaught; and built a church at this place, called Kill-Aladh, over which he placed one of his disciples, St Muredach, as bishop.

The cathedral's own signage points out that the pagan King Awley (Amolgid or Amalghaidh mac Fiachrach), who gave his name to the Barony of Tirawley, donated the land to Patrick.

According to Tírechán, Patrick was at Tara helping the High King Loegaire judge in a land dispute between the seven sons of Amolgid. When he discovered Enda, son of Amolgid, was from the Wood of Foclut in the west, he was overjoyed because he knew he was meant to go there. Enda did not want Patrick to come with him for fear the people would turn on them and kill them. But Patrick insisted and eventually he relented. However he judged it wiser for he and his brothers to wait for baptism until they had spoken to the people themselves.

In 1898, workmen discovered a circular chamber with a bee-hive roof and two passages leading off to the east and the west. This elaborate structure shows that there was an ancient rath, or fort, on the site, and the original Patrician church was probably built within it.

'THE WOOD OF FOCLUT BY THE WESTERN SEA'

Patrick himself says he was called back to Ireland in a dream:

I saw in my dream a man coming to me from Ireland, whose name was Victoricus, with a great number of letters...While I was reading [them] I thought for a moment I was hearing the voice of those near the Wood of Foclut by the Western Sea, and they cried 'We entreat thee, holy youth, to come and walk among us'...

This 'Wood of Foclut' may be Foghill (Fochaill) near Kil-lala Bay. It is the only Irish placename Patrick mentions in his writing, and conflicting theories abound about this. Many scholars maintain that this, rather than Slemish, is the place of Patrick's captivity and where he was drawn back to when he returned to Ireland. It is certainly true that the whole area was wooded at the time, as he describes and as the name suggests, and it is also true that it is by a western sea, that is, the Atlantic.

There is a St Patrick's Well at Foghill, which is also known as Tobar na Craoibhe (Well of the Branch). A local story says that two young women had helped Patrick when he was on the run from slavery, and that he built them a church on the spot where they had previously worshipped pagan gods, which was formerly known as Tulach na nDruadh, or Place of the Druids.

DOWNPATRICK HEAD, COUNTY MAYO

Near the world's largest Stone Age monument of Céide Fields is the magnificent headland Downpatrick Head. Its main fea-

Dún Briste sea stack, Downpatrick Head, County Mayo

tures are a dramatic sea stack, Dún Briste (the Broken Fort), and an extremely scary blowhole, Poll na Seantainne.

As with all sea stacks and blowholes, Dún Briste and Poll na Seantainne have been shaped by wind and water erosion. They crop up regularly in history. It is recorded that in 1393, during a series of fierce storms, the breach between Dún Briste and the mainland became complete – and people stranded had to be evacuated by rope bridges. Four hundred years later, Poll na Seantainne was being used as a hiding place by the insurgents of the 1798 Rebellion. But when the tide came in, it flooded the blowhole and drowned them.

One ancient story tells how the pagan god, Crom Dubh, lived on the headland and lit his fire on the spot of Poll na Seantainne. When he refused to convert to Christianity, Patrick threw a wooden crucifix into Crom's fire and it burned through solid rock, making a deep hole straight through to the raging sea below. Crom Dubh then retreated to the edge of the cliff, whereupon Patrick struck the ground with his crozier. The stack was instantly broken off from the mainland – hence the name – and Crom Dubh left to die a lonely death upon it. Other stories about Dún Briste are recounted by local schoolchildren and displayed on an information board nearby.

Patrick founded one of his many churches at Downpatrick Head, though the ruins are hard to find. There is, however, an instantly recognisable statue of the saint erected in the early 1980s. The saint has his back to the wonderful views over the cliffs, and instead gazes inland, into the homes and hearts of his flock.

WHAT THE CHILDREN SAY

At Downpatrick Head, there is a display of versions of the story of Downpatrick by local children. These imaginative re-tellings are likely handed down from older family members and they're a great example of how some elements of the story remain constant – and how some are improved by the teller.

According to one seven-year-old:

Geodruise, an ogre, lived on the head. He would make life difficult for St Patrick who liked to pray at the church. The saint became mad and prayed that God put a barrier between the ogre and himself. The following morning the stack with the ogre was separated from the mainland.

And another:

The arch [connecting the stack to the headland] collapsed and the people were stranded on the top. They escaped by weaving the thatch from the cottage roofs, and climbed down to curraghs waiting to rescue them.

And this from a six-year-old:

A robber lived at the headland and stole some of Patrick's cattle. When Patrick asked for them back the robber wouldn't listen and drove St Patrick away. That night St Patrick asked God to separate the robber from other people, and that night a portion of cliff was parted from the mainland with the robber still on it.

And finally, from a nine-year-old:

A long time ago there was a giant that lived near Down-patrick Head. Everyone in the area was afraid of him so St Patrick helped them. He chased the giant to the edge and then waited till he was asleep. Then he struck the ground with his staff and part of Downpatrick broke away. This left the giant stranded and unable to scare or harm the people of Ballycastle.

RIVER DUFF, ANCIENT BORDER

Along with the River Drowes, the River Duff forms part of the old border between the provinces of Connacht and Ulster. When Patrick crossed from Sligo into Leitrim, legend says that he cursed the river because local fishermen refused him fish. He reversed the curse when two boys shared their catch with him. Nearby is Patrick's Well and the Shaving Well – perhaps where they shaved off their hair to make tonsures.

PATRICK'S CURSES

It didn't do to cross Patrick. He cursed individuals, but also rivers, mountains and fields. He called down plagues and 'foreign dom-ination' on entire tribes. And his curses were usually tailor-made: For obstinate chieftains who wouldn't convert, his curses included children who would kill each other, or having drunk or deformed descendants, unfit for rule. Uppity druids were cursed with losing their memory or being mocked in an assembly. Farmers were cursed with bad weather, and warriors with defeat in battle.

DEAD OR ALIVE

There are a number of stories about Patrick, which involve death or near-death, followed by a Lazarus-like resurrection. One story involves a prince known as Maccul.

Maccul wished to test the supposed miraculous powers of Patrick. He gathered his supporters together and ordered one young man to play dead under a shroud. If Patrick was truly a miracle worker, claimed Maccul, he would instantly know the shrouded person was alive not dead.

When Patrick arrived he headed straight for the young man, loudly chanting the prayers for his entry to Heaven.

'Aha!' said Maccul, 'I have you now, you fraud! Look under the shroud!'

But when Patrick lifted the shroud, the young man was indeed dead. The appalled prince fell on his knees, and Patrick relented and brought the man back to life. But the penalty for Maccul was severe. He was to be shackled and set adrift in a boat. Fortunately for him, he washed up on the Isle of Man, where he eventually became a bishop.

Sometimes people died and stayed dead. There is a famous story about the two daughters of the high king Loegaire, Eithne and Fidelma, who met Patrick at a well near the hill fort of Rathcroghan. They questioned the saint about Jesus, and were so impressed with his answers that they implored him to baptise them. Patrick did so and the sisters immediately died in an enviable, perfect state of sinless purity – not a fate expected to apply to young male converts!

VALLEY OF THE KINGS: STORIES FROM LEINSTER

It is logical to assume that the adult Patrick made first landfall on the island of Ireland around 432. According to the earliest biographers, this happened on the east coast near the mouth of the River Boyne, or further south where Wicklow now stands (though current thinking is that County Down in the northeast was a more likely landing place). Leinster is a landscape rich in pagan culture with standing stones, henges and sacred waters. There is a wealth of archaeology in the valley of the Boyne, including ancient graves, and the famous hill of Tara was once the power base of the High King of Ireland. Further afield, the age-old custom of the Lughnasa fire festival can still be witnessed at Uisneach, the sacred centre of pre-Christian Ireland.

INVER DÉ, COUNTY WICKLOW

This is where both Muirchú and Tírechán claim Patrick disembarked at the very beginning of his mission. According to the *Leabhar Breac*, he found a great welcome from a local chieftain. A little boy in the house became so devoted to Patrick that he begged to travel with him on his journey. So his family agreed, and the boy, Benignus, went on to be the first native Irishman to become a bishop.

WICKLOW, COUNTY WICKLOW

An alternative legend claims that when Patrick first attempted to land in Wicklow near the estuary of the River Vartry, warlike locals repelled him and smashed the teeth of one of his followers, giving the place its ancient Irish name Cill Mhantáin or Church of the Toothless One. However, this incident is more likely to have happened to Palladius, Patrick's predecessor (see Pack of Pats, page 19), since he is recorded as having had a hostile reception when first in Ireland.

DID YOU KNOW?

During the nineteenth century, Queen Victoria banned her Irish regiments from wearing the shamrock anywhere on their uniform. The plant had become associated with constitutional nationalism, of which she was not a fan. But after heavy losses in Irish regiments during the Boer War, she changed her mind.

SHAM SHAMROCK?

One of the most famous stories about Patrick is how he picked a three-leaved shamrock to explain his religion. But today's plant is not the same as the one Patrick knew. The early edible plant was trefoil wood sorrel, a native to Ireland. Nowadays this native plant has been replaced by another clover – inedible this time – that has been in Ireland since the sixteenth century. It is said that Patrick used the famous three leaves on one stalk to explain the Christian idea of the Trinity – Father, Son and Holy Spirit – the three parts making up one God. However the first mention of Patrick's link with the shamrock wasn't until 1727!

THE HILL OF UISNEACH, COUNTY WESTMEATH

Near to Ballymore, Uisneach packs a lot into a relatively small hill. Archaeology shows it had been a ritual site for the burning of sacred fires since Neolithic times. The turn of the seasons and the life-giving sun were celebrated here, along with pagan deities, such as Eriu, who gave her name to Ireland.

It was the site of the great festival of Bealtaine, when a massive ritual fire was lit that could be seen for miles around. Here too Lughnasa, the harvest festival, was celebrated at the end of August. The god who gave his name to this festival, the famous Lugh of the Long Arm, ruled from here and died here. Another

The Hill of Uisneach still hosts the pre-Christian festivals of Bealtaine and Lughnasa

legend says that the god Nemhedh fought and banished the giant Formorians from here.

Before Tara, Uisneach was the seat of the high kings. Great royal assemblies were held here. In Brehon times, these were not optional party invitations. A cattle fine would be imposed on those who failed to turn up wearing their best clothes and jewels. The king would use the assemblies to make judgements in cases of land dispute, and offer lavish hospitality to vassals, in return for their continuing loyalty.

Located at the centre of Meath (Midhe, the 'middle' fifth province of Ireland), Uisneach also marks the exact centre of Ireland, the 'navel of the land' – though how ancient people would have sensed this is not clear. The area is covered with fascinating ancient features including forts, cairns, earthworks, and even an ancient chariot road connecting east and west. There is an enormous boulder known as the Catstone (Aill na Míreann) where the goddess Eriu is said to be buried.

Uisneach's current signage reads:
- Site of Celtic festival of Bealtaine [celebrated 1 May]
- Ancient place of assembly
- St Patrick's Church
- Sacred centre of Ireland in pagan times
- Site of druidic fire cult
- Seat of high kings

Small wonder then that Patrick headed for this sacred place to found a church. It was not plain sailing: he was repelled by the dominant clan at the time, the O'Neills, and he placed a curse on the stones of Uisneach.

The site also features in a work first written down from older oral sources in the thirteenth century called the *Colloquy with the Ancients* (Agallamh na Seanórach). This is part of the Fenian cycle of myths from pre-Christian times, in which Caoílte, a giant warrior of Fionn mac Cumhaill's Fianna, meets with Patrick and the King of Ireland and tells them the legends of the past.

There is a St Patrick's Bed at Uisneach, which is a stone that marks the spot where Brigid met Patrick. There is also a St Patrick's Church and a St Patrick's Well.

BRIGID: SLAVE, GODDESS, PRIEST AND NUN

Brigid, one of Ireland's most loved saints, is a semi-historical figure based, in part, on an older pagan goddess of the same name.

The goddess Brigid was the daughter of the Dagda, king of the gods. The pagan Irish called upon her help to heal the sick and comfort the dying, and also to look after the all-important livestock. Her feast day in early February was known as Imbolc and it celebrated the moment when the winter gave way to the first promise of spring.

The historical St Brigid has melded with this earlier goddess figure. Tradition says that her father, Dubhthach, was a druid (or a chieftain in some versions), and her mother, Broicsech, his slave. Young Brigid grew up in Faughart, County Louth, where her charity, healing and miracles made her famous.

One story says that Brigid took holy orders from Patrick at Uisneach. During the vows, Patrick used the form of words

Joseph Edward Nuttgens'
1952 window of St Brigid,
featuring the cattle and crops
with which she was associated,
in the Church of St Etheldreda,
central London.

reserved for priests, not nuns. When it was pointed out to him he said, 'Let it stand', recognising perhaps that she was a formidable personality. Indeed she went on to become the foremost Christian leader in Leinster, and is credited with converting many women, including important pagan princesses.

Tradition says that Brigid remained such a friend to Patrick that they were called the 'twin pillars' of the early church. Patrick and his successors knew well what they were doing; the people who had always loved the goddess Brigid and called on her help were able to continue to do so in her new guise of St Brigid.

St Brigid travelled widely and founded a number of religious houses, much bigger at the time than any monastery run by men. There are a number of overlaps between the saint and the goddess. The saint's most famous convent, housing both men and women at Kildare, was on a pagan site previously devoted to the goddess (Cill Dara means Church of the Oak Tree, a pre-Christian sacred tree). Another overlap may relate to her symbol, St Brigid's cross. Do the spokes radiating from the centre represent the pagan sun turned into a Christian symbol? Finally St Brigid's feast day is celebrated on 1 February – at the same time as Imbolc, the festival of her pagan namesake.

PATRICK AND THE ASSASSIN OF KILDARE

The *Tripartite Life* says that as Patrick passed through Kildare, he escaped an assassination attempt due to the loyalty of Odhran, his charioteer.

Failge Berraide, one of the pagan lords of the area, had boasted that if he met Patrick he would kill him, in revenge for the overthrow of the idol Crom Cruaich, which had been specially venerated by Failge. His murderous boast was concealed from Patrick by his people, but when they all came into Failge's district, Odhran the charioteer took matters into his own hands.

Said Odhran to the saint, 'Since I have been a long time driving for you, Patrick, let me take the chief seat for this day, and you be the charioteer.' Patrick consented, and changed positions with Odhran. After this Failge came up and stabbed Odhran, believing him to be Patrick. In one version of this story, Patrick curses Failge but Odhran begs Patrick with his dying breath to place the curse instead on a tree sacred to Failge's clan. This Patrick did and Odhran, at the moment of his death, forgave his murderer, becoming the only martyr in Patrick's time.

SKERRIES, COUNTY DUBLIN

This 'rocky place' on the east coast has a group of three uninhabited islands, Inishpatrick, Colt Island and Red Island, which are linked with Patrick.

According to Tírechán, Inishpatrick (St Patrick's Island) was visited by Patrick when he first came back to Ireland. A story relates how one day, while he was out preaching, the mainlanders came to Inishpatrick and stole his goat, which they cooked and ate. When Patrick came after the thieves, he jumped from Inishpatrick onto Red Island where his footprint can still be seen to this day. A local tradition is to put three fingers into the water in the footprint and make a wish.

Another story says that Inishpatrick was where he stopped overnight when sailing north from Wicklow to Down to see his old master.

ST PATRICK'S CATHEDRAL, DUBLIN CITY

This beautiful Church of Ireland cathedral is one of the largest churches in Ireland. It is medieval, but was founded on the site of a pre-Christian spring, in which Patrick baptised converts around 450.

Stone in St Patrick's Cathedral showing the Celtic cross. It is believed to be from a well where Patrick conducted baptisms.

St Patrick's Cathedral, Dublin, c. 1890–1900

A slab can still be seen from that time, featuring an early Celtic cross, which was used to cover the sacred well.

The Order of St Patrick, whose regalia can be seen hanging around the cathedral, is a dormant chivalric order, that is, a social club for knights of the realm. Chivalric orders were created by monarchs all over Europe and this one was started by George III in 1783 to prop up the Protestant Ascendancy, and give the wealthy a reason to dress up. The insignia, a type of jewelled badge, was so ornate it was also known as the Irish Crown Jewels. It was stolen from Dublin Castle just before a royal visit in 1907, and never seen again.

FROM MYTHS TO MONKS: STORIES FROM MUNSTER

Truth was in our hearts,

Strength was in our arms,

And what we said, we fulfilled.

Caoílte mac Rónáin, a warrior of the Fianna

Before the Christian Era, there was much movement on the seas between Ireland and Spain, France, Britain and beyond. Because of this sea contact, there were already monasteries in the south before Patrick came, set up by Ciaran, Declan, Ailbe and Ibar.

But Patrick gained a major feather in his mitre when he made a high-profile royal conversion at the Rock of Cashel. Cashel was connected to the royal hill of Tara via a gap between Slievenamon and Slieveardagh – an important interface for Leinster and Munster, and for paganism and the spread of Christianity.

The mythological band of warriors, the Fianna, feature in many tales about Patrick and there are lively stories about when the two traditions – mythical and monkish – came face to face.

THE COLLOQUY WITH THE ANCIENTS

A famous version of a meeting between Patrick and the mythological heroes of the Fianna was written down for the first time in the thirteenth century from oral sources and is one of the most important parts of the Fenian cycle of tales in Irish.

In Standish Hayes O'Grady's description of *The Colloquy with the Ancients*, Patrick is going about his business when nine of the Fianna emerge out of the mist to meet him. They are giants and the 'largest man of the Christians reached but to the waist of any one of the others'.

Through this story, Patrick is an interested and appreciative audience. A hero named Caoílte mac Rónáin, a nephew of Fionn mac Cumhall, walks with Patrick and tells him of the glories of the pagan past. For example, to be accepted as part of the warrior band one had to pass the following severe tests of worthiness:

- He must be buried to his middle in the earth, and must, with a shield and a hazel stick, defend himself against nine warriors casting spears at him, and if he were wounded he was not accepted.
- He must race through the forest, chased by the Fians. If he were overtaken, or if a braid of his hair were disturbed, or if a dry stick cracked under his foot, he was not accepted.
- He must be able to leap over a lath level with his brow and to run at full speed under a lath level with his knee.
- He must be able, while running, to draw out a thorn from his foot and never slacken speed.
- He must be skilled in making verse.
- He must demand no dowry with a wife.

Patrick asks many questions about the Fianna. Was Fionn mac Cumhaill a good lord? How many fosterlings had he? How many horses and hounds? Were there golden drinking cups in the Fianna's hall? And how was it that the Fianna became so mighty and so glorious that all Ireland sang of their deeds? Famously Caoílte answers, 'Truth was in our hearts; strength was in our arms; and what we said, we fulfilled.'

Caoílte expands. He tells stories of how Fionn located his lost hounds by putting his thumb in his mouth to his tooth of knowledge. He explains the genealogy of characters, such as Goll mac Morna. He even takes him to a water source so he can baptise the people, a mythical and beautiful lough named Trá Dá Bhan (Two Women's Strand).

He describes to Patrick how Oisín, the son of Fionn Mac Cumhall, was so generous that if a man had nothing 'only a head to eat with', he would give him anything he wanted. He tells tales of some of the vividly named warriors of the Fianna – Raighne the wide-eyed, Cael the hundred-slayer, Conall the slaughterer, Eoghan red-weapon, and others. He repeats the life lesson Fionn had given to a young warrior:

> Beat not thy hound…
> Bring not a charge against thy wife,
> In battle meddle not with a buffoon…
> Two thirds of thy gentleness be shown
> To women and to creepers on the floor,
> Likewise to men of art…
> And be not violent to the common people…
> Hasten not to be the first into bed…
> Utter not swaggering speech…
> Neither for gold nor for other earthly valuables
> Abandon thou thy guarantee.
>
> From Hayes O'Grady's translation, *1000 Years of Irish Poetry*

For his part Patrick is keen to convert the heroes, but first he needs to check with his angels that he can continue to talk with them. The angels agree that he can, pointing out that the heroes' stories are important. They have already forgotten two-thirds of what they know, say the angels, and saving the rest will offer a pastime for generations to come (which indeed it has). Patrick then gets his scribe Brogan to write down as many stories as he can.

CASHEL OF THE KINGS

A prominent outcrop of limestone in the lush Golden Vale of Tipperary, the Rock of Cashel (*caiseal* meaning stone fort) has been an important fortified position since at least the fourth century.

According to local mythology, the Rock originated in a mountain 30 kilometres (19 miles) away, which is known as the Devil's Bit. One version has it that the mountain was so called because it features a large nick, which is where the Devil took a bite out of it. The bite of rock broke the Devil's tooth. Furious, he spat it out, and it landed where the Cashel is today. Another version of the story has it that Patrick forced the Devil to spit the rock, as he banished him from his mountain stronghold.

The formal name for Cashel is St Patrick's Rock (Carraig Phádraig), while informally the place is also called Cashel of the Kings. This relates to the fact that, for centuries, the Rock was the stronghold of the overkings of Munster. Lesser kings, of Thomond and Ossory, for example, answered to this powerful ruler, while he answered only to the King at Tara.

The Rock of Cashel, County Tipperary, c. 1905, a stronghold of the early kings of Munster

Patrick travelled to Cashel around 445 to respond to a request by King Aengus to be baptised. During the ceremony, which took place on the Rock in front of all the court and assembled vassals, there was an unfortunate incident, which shows the stoical nature of Aengus. Patrick drove his crozier into the ground to free up his hands – and accidentally skewered Aengus's foot with the sharp end. The poor man did and said nothing, and it was only afterwards that Patrick realised what he'd done. He asked Aengus why he'd endured such pain without complaint, to which Aengus replied that he had thought it was part of the baptism ritual! According to the *Leabhar Breac*, Patrick proclaimed that no blood should be shed on Cashel from that day on. The crozier itself was famously beautiful (see Raholp, page 110).

OISÍN IN PATRICK'S HOUSE

The Irish playwright and folklorist, Lady Augusta Gregory (1852–1932), tells the story of when Patrick met Oisín. In one version this happened near Cashel, but the story is claimed by other regions too.

Oisín is loved by Niamh of the Golden Hair, a fairy princess of Tír na nÓg, and taken back with her to the magical land of eternal youth. But after three years Oisín is homesick and wants to see Ireland again. So Niamh allows him to go on her white horse on one condition: he must not under any circumstances dismount or touch the ground of Ireland, or he will never be able to return to her.

When Oisín reaches Ireland, he sees with sadness that his father's fort is all in ruins, and the people are speaking strangely. Slowly he realises he has not been away for three years, but for three hundred. While he is pondering this, he bends down to help some men lift a heavy stone at Cashel. The girth of his white horse snaps and he crashes to the ground. Immediately he ages and withers into a very, very old man.

Patrick is sent for and brings Oisín to his own home to look after him – and also to try and baptise him before he dies.

THE LEGENDS OF SLIEVENAMON

As Patrick and Caoílte journey through Ireland, they pass this 720-metre (2,362-foot) mountain. Caoílte tells how he and Fionn mac Cumhall and their comrades chased a fawn here from Ulster. The fawn leads them to a fairy fort housing twenty-eight heroes and twenty-eight maidens, where Fionn and his men are entertained lavishly. The fairies then ask them to fight another host of fairy folk due to attack that night. After Fionn's inevitable victory, he brokers a peace among the fairy people, and they lead his men back to the world. Caoílte's tale ends with the leader of the twenty-eight warriors, Donn, appearing out of nowhere and paying homage to Patrick.

FROM MYTHS TO MONKS

Many scholars believe there were Christians in the southwest and southeast before Patrick came. The most famous among these are called the 'Four Bishops': Declan, Ciaran, Ailbe and Ibar. An ancient text known as The Life of St Declan claims these monks, whose authority predated Patrick's, were dismayed to discover that Patrick was on his way to bring them to heel for Rome.

Declan of Ardmore (Waterford) had met Patrick as a student possibly in Rome and was on good terms with him, but was unwilling to acknowledge him as his superior – until told to by an angel. Ciaran of Saighir (Cork) could see how many of the great kings were being converted and acknowledged Patrick's leadership before he even met him. Ailbe of Emly (Tipperary) had enjoyed being seen by the other bishops as their leader, but chose to publicly humble himself in front of King Aengus at Cashel, and accept Patrick. And Ibar of Beg Eri (Wexford) was the most contrary of the four, unwilling to accept Patrick because he was a 'foreigner', having been born in Britain. Again an angelic mediator got involved and resolved the issue.

KNOCKPATRICK, COUNTY LIMERICK

The current church at Knockpatrick (Patrick's Hill), near Foynes, is 175 metres (572 feet) above sea level with gorgeous views over the Shannon Estuary. According to legend, Patrick consecrated an earlier church here in 448. There is also a holy well here. The *Tripartite Life* says that, because he never went into Kerry, Patrick blessed all that lay west of this spot.

To the east of the church there are six stones known as Suíochán Pádraig (Patrick's Seat). A local historian, Dr Mannix Joyce, recorded that the tradition of praying at Stations was carried out here. The Rosary was said while circling the stones, the churchyard and the holy well.

HAIL, PATRICK!

A traditional St Patrick's Day song is the famous hymn, 'Hail, Glorious St Patrick!' The origin of its melody is thought to be an ancient Gaelic air, but the lyrics were written by a nun, Sister Agnes, back in the mid-nineteenth century. Nothing is known about her, except that she lived in a Sisters of Mercy convent in Charleville, County Cork, yet her words have travelled all over the world. The hymn has been covered by The Wolfe Tones and Daniel O'Donnell in their own inimitable styles. With its reference to Irish exiles, it is still sung in many churches on St Patrick's Day.

> Hail, glorious St Patrick, dear saint of our isle,
> On us thy poor children bestow a sweet smile;
> And now thou art high in the mansions above,
> On Erin's green valleys, look down in thy love.

> *Chorus*
> On Erin's green valleys, on Erin's green valleys,
> On Erin's green valleys, look down in thy love.

> Thy people, now exiles on many a shore,
> Shall love and revere thee till time be no more;
> And the fire thou hast kindled shall ever burn bright,
> Its warmth undiminished, undying its light.

> *Chorus*

> Ever bless and defend the sweet land of our birth,
> Where the shamrock still blooms as when thou wert on earth,
> And our hearts shall yet burn, wherever we roam,
> For God and St Patrick, and our native home.

The following prayer, The Breastplate of St Patrick, was traditionally said to have been penned by Patrick himself and is set to music in many versions:

Christ be with me, Christ within me,
Christ behind me, Christ before me,
Christ beside me, Christ to win me,
Christ to comfort and restore me.
Christ beneath me, Christ above me,
Christ in quiet, Christ in danger ...

SAINT PATRICK WAS A GENTLEMAN

The first verse of this classic was retrieved from the memory of His Excellency Dan Mulhall, Ambassador of Ireland to the United Kingdom (2013–2017), and was sung by him on the occasion of the thirtieth anniversary of the Irish in Britain Archive at Metropolitan University, London, 22 November 2016.

St Patrick was a gentleman, he came from decent people;
In Dublin town he built a church and on it put a steeple.
His father was a Callaghan, his mother was a Brady,
His auntie an O'Shaughnessy, his uncle an O'Grady.

Chorus:
Then here's to bold St Paddy's fist, he was a saint so clever
He gave the snakes and toads a twist and banished them forever!

There's not a mile in Erin's isle where the dirty vermin musters,
Where'er he put his dear forefoot, he murdered them in clusters.
The toads went hop, the frogs went pop, slap dash into the water,
And beasts committed suicide to save themselves from slaughter!

Chorus

No wonder that those Irish lads should be so gay and frisky,
For sure, Saint Pat, he taught them that, as well as making whiskey!
No wonder that the saint himself should understand distilling,
His mother kept a shebeen shop in the town of Enniskillen.

Chorus

O! was I but so fortunate as to be back in Munster,
'Tis I'd be bound that, from that ground,
I never more would once stir,
For there St Patrick planted turf, and plenty of the praties
With pigs galore, mo grá, mo'sthore, and cabbages – and ladies!

PART FOUR

THE GREENING OF THE WORLD

Previous page: Dublin's famous General Post Office

This page: Rio de Janeiro's colossal statue of Christ the Redeemer

P atrick's festival on 17 March has changed from a one-day religious commemoration to a worldwide phenomenon lasting, in some cases, several weeks. In the nineteenth century, the idea of marking St Patrick's Day by enjoying Irish traditional song and dance travelled with Irish immigrants to America – and then, like themed pubs and Halloween, it was changed and successfully re-imported back to Ireland. The Global Greening initiative by Tourism Ireland has enormously boosted Ireland's international profile with hundreds of the world's most iconic sights lit green every year in celebration of St Patrick's Day.

SPECIAL RELATIONSHIP: USA

Erin's son to western empire,
Westward takes his star and course,
To the land of freedom's campfire,
Brings his energies and force,
He is welcome to adopt
Our stars and stripes, his flag, to be,
But his love, he still with fervour,
Sends across the Atlantic Sea.

Erin's Vacant Chair, AJ Seabrook

Over four centuries it is estimated that four million Irish immigrants to the USA have grown to forty million Irish-Americans. Today throughout all states of America there are

Immigrants arriving at Ellis Island, New York Harbor

museums, monuments and other sites commemorating the material culture of the Irish and the contributions they have made to American life.

As well as a number of inventions (for example, the first US Navy submarines by Clare man John Holland), Irish-Americans are also responsible for one major aspect of American popular culture as we know it in the twenty-first century: St Patrick's Day.

As we now know, the original and ancient springtime pagan fertility rite in Ireland was Bealtaine, which centred on placating the deities of sowing and fertility and pre-dated the Christian springtime festival of Easter by many hundreds of years. As Christianity took hold in Ireland, bolstered by the cult of its most lauded advocate, the anniversary of his death became more important, but back then it was a day of fasting, not celebration. Later it was made a 'holy day of obligation', which meant obligatory mass attendance. It became a much bigger festival among the Irish Diaspora than it was back home in Ireland.

For generations in Ireland, then, fasting and mass-going were the quiet, religious observances of St Patrick's Day. But, along with millions of Irish immigrants, St Patrick's Day arrived in the United States, and became the cherished custom of millions

An Irish-American mother pins shamrock to her son's lapel in this 1870s print.

SAINT PATRICK

more Americans. It has been re-invented by them and their descendants as a celebratory day of all things Irish, becoming more secular in the process. The land of opportunity, with paid work and material benefits replacing landlordism and starvation, changed the quiet sobriety and religiousness of the original festival into one where being proud to be Irish was on display.

And just like Irish pubs and Irish dancing, St Patrick's Day has been re-packaged and commercialised and re-exported all over the world – especially back to Ireland. It is now one of the world's biggest festivals.

WHO STARTED IT?

In 1737 St Patrick's Day social gatherings took place in Boston when a group of well-to-do Irish-Americans hosted extravagant

Flag bearers at the St Patrick's Day Parade at the corner of 5th Avenue and East 64th Street, New York City.

lunches for each other across taverns in the city. The marching tradition, with parades, floats and music, didn't start until 1762 with New York City's first recorded St Patrick's Day parade. Today the New York parade travels along 5th Avenue from 44th Street up to 79th Street. It includes hundreds of thousands of marchers and bands and is watched by thousands on the day and millions more on TV. It has become a major annual spectacle and is the largest parade in the world.

DID YOU KNOW?

For several years from 1997, a village called Dripsey in County Cork, hosted the world's shortest Patrick's Day parade. It was 23 metres (75 feet) long – the distance between two village pubs. When one of the pubs closed, the title was taken by Hot Springs in Arkansas, which boasts a parade of just under 30 metres (98 feet).

EAT YOUR GREENS

As the saying goes, 'There are two kinds of people on St Patrick's Day – those who are Irish and those who wish they were Irish.'

These days, all around the USA, everything goes green from buildings to clothes to people. Large and small merchandise is available, from books and films to green bikinis. You can even install a stained glass window decoration in your home featuring the man himself.

Special St Patrick's Day food appears in the form of shamrock shakes and green bread. Restaurants do a roaring trade with corned beef and cabbage – an Irish-American re-interpretation

A New York high school band takes to 5th Avenue for the St Patrick's Day parade.

of the traditional dish bacon and cabbage. And we must not forget the 'drowning of the shamrock' – either in green beer, or in spirits, honouring one of the myths associated with Patrick that he brought the skill of distilling whiskey to Ireland.

Although the New York parade is the daddy of them all, with upwards of 200,000 marchers and one million spectators annually, there are cities all over America that hold their own parades, concerts, fairs and fundraisers, and this generates income for those communities. The festivities also generate income for Ireland, as Irish tourism receives an enormous boost at this time of year.

Some argue that this commercialisation means the festival is no longer an Irish, or even Irish-American festival, but a fully American festival. It has been transformed from a religious and cultural event into both a business opportunity and a political one. In fact, to fit all this in, St Patrick's Day has now become St Patrick's Season and it can last up to two weeks. Indeed, in the USA, March has been Irish-American heritage month since 1991.

DID YOU KNOW?

Blue, not green, was the original colour associated with Patrick and with Ireland. In fact, the modern Irish Presidential Standard is a golden harp on an azure (blue) field.

POLITICAL ANIMALS

The New York parade always had a political dimension. The Irish-Americans that took part in it were not only congratulating themselves for doing well in public service and in political office, but also demonstrating patriotism and gratitude to America for making this possible. There are always stars and stripes visible in the parade, often carried by patriotic representatives of traditional Irish-American jobs, such as the New York police and fire departments.

Ireland sends its politicians abroad on St Patrick's Day to make diplomatic connections, and it is the Taoiseach (Irish prime minister) who goes to the US. The first US president to attend the New York St Patrick's Day parade was Harry Truman in 1948, in the hope of courting Irish-American voters, and every St Patrick's Day since 1952, the Taoiseach has presented the US president with a bunch of shamrock in a Waterford crystal bowl. Nowadays it would be unthinkable for the mayor of New

York, or indeed any politician seeking election not to attend St Patrick's Day events.

The festivities around St Patrick's Day can be an opportunity for serious diplomacy, such as in 1996 when some of the Northern Ireland peace talks took place in Washington during the festival.

Band leader Benny Goodman and dancer Eunice Healy celebrate St Patrick's Day with two Irish-American senators on the steps of the Capitol, Washington DC, 1939.

In 2002, just six months after the atrocity of 9/11, the New York parade was dedicated to all victims of terror – Christian, Muslim, Jewish and other faiths or none. Firefighters and police bands turned out en masse, and the St Patrick's Day parade became an event about American brotherhood.

PROTESTANT AND CATHOLIC

In the eighteenth century, Irish migrants to the USA were usually non-conformist Protestants, such as Ulster Presbyterians, who were under the same Penal Laws as Catholics, and who left Ireland to practise their faith in freedom. In the nineteenth century, this demographic dramatically changed; Irish migrants were now predominantly Catholics fleeing oppression and starvation, particularly the Great Famine and its miserable aftermath. The resulting melting pot was beneficial; Irish-American communities, whether religious or not, have often worked together for common goals.

These days, the New York parade still pauses for prayer outside St Patrick's Roman Catholic Cathedral on 5th Avenue. But Catholicism can go hand-in-hand with conservatism and there is now a growing gap between the more inclusive approach of younger attendees and the 'traditional family values' of the older attendees and organisers.

For example, for many years, gays and lesbians were not allowed to march under banners, only as individuals in the New York parade. Controversy about this non-inclusivity bubbled for decades, ending up in court several times, where judges tended to rule against the LGBTQ+ groups. This situation continued

New York's 5th Avenue filled with LGBTQ+ protesters during the parade of 2015.

until 2015 when a non-Irish gay group associated with the televising of the parade finally marched under their own banner.

NOT QUITE ACCORDING TO PLAN ...

For some, the festival in America was an opportunity for exuberance in the matter of alcoholic consumption. In his 1868 book, *The Irish in America,* John Francis Maguire, MP for Cork, offered this extraordinary generalisation:

> The Americans drink, the Germans drink, the Scotch drink, the English drink – all drink with more or less injury to their health or circumstances, but whatever the injury ... it is far greater to the mercurial and light-hearted Irish, than to races of hard head

and lethargic temperament. The Irishman is by nature averse to solitary or selfish indulgence – he will not 'booze' in secret, or make himself drunk from a mere love of liquor; with him the indulgence is the more fascinating when it enhances the pleasures of friendship, and imparts additional zest to the charms of social intercourse …

But the consumption of food and drink on St Patrick's Day is rooted in history. It is traditionally one day of allowable excess in Lent, the six-week abstinence marathon leading up to Easter.

There is a long history of unexpected incidents occurring on 17 March, including riot, injuries and natural disasters.

A New York newspaper carries a report on an the attack on the police at the corner of Grand and Pitt Streets, New York City in 1867.

- In 1870, one Thomas Macdonald of 124th Street was passing in front of City Hall, New York, when he was shot in the leg by a discharge of the cannon, which was firing the salute in honour of the day.
- In 1904 during the New York Parade, two boys managed to jump on horses belonging to the marshals of the Ancient Order of Hibernians. They galloped for about six blocks, pursued by police, before dismounting and escaping on foot.
- In 1908, 150 students at Georgetown, Washington State, rioted when they were refused permission for a holiday on St Patrick's Day. They turned a hose on their teachers, including a Jesuit priest. As a result, thirty students were expelled and 120 suspended.
- In 1936, a combination of melting snow and rainfall on St Patrick's Day caused massive flooding and claimed more than sixty lives in western Pennsylvania.
- On St Patrick's Day in 2014, an earthquake in Los Angeles was televised live on a news show.

PATRICK'S DAY PAGANISM

The historian Roy Foster in the *New York Times* (2003) claimed that the New York St Patrick's Day parade is 'a carnival celebrating the end of winter' as much as anything else. Thus we come full circle to what was certainly the case in Patrick's time – a collective sigh of relief and a burst of good spirits on having struggled through the death of winter to the new life of spring. Today, many festival-goers are not first- or second-generation Irish. Many have mixed heritage and feel proud to be able to

Youthful enthusiasm for St Patrick's Day

celebrate every aspect of that. Many have weak or even no Irish ties. None of this matters on St Patrick's Day in the US. What matters is to feel Irish for the day, join in the fun and show solidarity with your fellow Americans.

DID YOU KNOW?

According to Hallmark, twelve million Americans exchange cards each year on St Patrick's Day.

THE BEST OF THE REST

AUSTRALIA

One of the major territories of the migration of Irish people has been Australia – but in the past they didn't always go willingly.

In the eighteenth and early nineteenth centuries, Australia was a penal colony used to hold convicted prisoners from Britain. The crimes that warranted transportation could be as minor as stealing handkerchiefs or bread. On the plus side, there was a chance you could earn your freedom after seven years; on the minus side, most people expected to be white bones in the red Australian earth before that time was up. Transportation reached its peak in the early-1800s, and many of those sentenced to transportation were Irish in Britain.

An Irish folk band in Brisbane, Australia, taking part in St Patrick's Day festivities in 2011. Australia has marked the occasion since 1810.

In Sydney, St Patrick's Day was first marked in 1810, when Lachlan Macquarie, the governor of New South Wales, provided entertainment for some of these Irish convict workers. Today, it is estimated that about 35 percent of Australians identify as Irish or of Irish descent, and many are delighted to find a colourful convict or two in their ancestry. There are three St Patrick's Cathedrals in Australia, one St Patrick's Basilica and at least half a dozen St Patrick's parish churches.

In 2010, the Sydney Opera House went green to mark the two-hundredth anniversary of Sydney's St Patrick's Day.

CANADA

St Patrick's Day is a public holiday in the province of Newfoundland and Labrador, which is still proud of its Irish character after

The Gaelic Athletic Association Montreal Shamrocks in the Montreal Saint Patrick's Day Parade (Défilé Saint-Patrick de Montréal) along Saint Catherine Street.

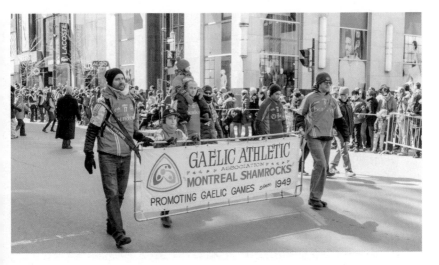

four hundred years of immigration. The St Patrick's Day Parade in Montreal is one of the oldest in North America, dating back to 1824.

ENGLAND

There is a small town in northwest Cumbria named Aspatria, which is on the route of a Roman road. There has been a settlement here for over 3,000 years, and it is one of the possible locations of Patrick's birth. A local story goes that Patrick was visiting his relatives down in Ravenglass to the south of the region. At this place, he preached so long that his ash staff, which he'd driven into the ground, took root, giving the place its name, 'the place of Patrick's ash tree'. Cumbria also has a St Patrick's Church in a town named Patterdale.

The pretty town of Glastonbury in Somerset has a long-standing claim to be the burial place of Patrick, though the stories are

Glastonbury Abbey, Somerset, which lays claim to be Patrick's burial place

more likely to be about Palladius (see A Pack of Patricks, page 19). There is a St Patrick's Chapel in part of Glastonbury Abbey.

Consecrated in 1792, St Patrick's Church in Soho in London was the first Catholic church in England (since the Reformation) to be dedicated to St Patrick. It was also one of the first Catholic parish churches established after the passing of the Catholic Relief Acts of the eighteenth century, which brought freedom of worship to London's poor Catholics after many years of discrimination. The area around this church was part of an Irish slum known as the Rookeries, which was rife with prostitution and was known locally as 'Tipperary'. In a wonderful double entendre set to music, the famous soldier's song 'It's a Long Way to Tipperary' is about a longing for the fleshpots of Soho, rather than homesickness for Ireland:

It's a long way to Tipperary, it's a long way to go,
It's a long way to Tipperary, to the sweetest girl I know,
Goodbye Piccadilly, farewell Leicester Square,
It's a long, long way to Tipperary, but my heart lies there.

FRANCE

There are several associations with Patrick in France, and he is thought to have undertaken his religious training here. There was certainly communication between Ireland and France by sea from the earliest times; one traditional sea route was between modern-day Wexford on the southeast coast of Ireland and northern Normandy, which is echoed today in the Rosslare Harbour–Cherbourg ferry service.

The Loire River at sunset

It is said that Patrick spent one winter preaching up and down the Loire Valley. One day Patrick went fishing in the river without permission. Angry local tribesmen ganged up and chased Patrick, who made his escape by swimming across the river towards a village today called Saint-Patrice. Now soaked, he spread his cape out to dry on a blackthorn bush and crawled into a small cave to rest. When he awoke, it was Christmas Day and there was snow on the ground. But when he took his cape from the blackthorn bush, it had flowered. A year later the miracle reccurred, and the bush flowered for many more years.

ISLE OF MAN

Around the time that Patrick was struggling in slavery (in the early years of the fifth century), Irish seafarers started to take over the Isle of Man. The island is thought to have been converted to Christianity by Maccul (or Maughold, d. 498), an Irish prince who was first an opponent and then a disciple of Patrick.

In a field called Magher-y-Chairn, in the parish of Marown, are three prehistoric standing stones known locally in the Manx language as Chairn-y-Pherick (meaning 'St Patrick's Chair'). Originally five were standing but two of the slabs have fallen; another two have intricate seventh- to ninth-century Christian crosses carved on them.

Local legend says that Patrick himself used the stones as a seat to preach from. But it is more likely that the location was a favoured preaching spot used by his successors. One of these successors was an Irish bishop called St Ronan, known locally as St Runius or Runy, who came after Maccul. It was he who founded a very early, tiny chapel (or *keeill* in Manx), near Chairn-y-Pherick. In the same field as St Patrick's Chair is a holy well called Chibber-y-Chairn (Well of the Chair), also known as St Ronan's Well.

IRELAND

Happy St Patrick's Day! Or 'Lá Fhéile Pádraig Sona Duit', as they say in Irish.

These days St Patrick's Day in Ireland sees a host of family-friendly festivities over the whole week, and the day itself is a national holiday. There are sporting events, concerts and fun activities, and performers and revellers fly in from around the world. Dublin's parade is a vibrant, inclusive affair that processes down O'Connell Street and across the O'Connell Bridge. There's a celebration of Irish food and drink with restaurants and bars doing a roaring trade.

But, until the 1960s, the experience was very different. Most pubs were closed for the day. In fact, for most of the twentieth century, St Patrick's Day in Ireland was somewhat dreary when compared with today – not to mention 'dry'. Repeated attempts by the Free State government in the 1920s to make it 'wet' were generally crushed by the Senate. Entertainment included military parades and the country's biggest dog show.

There were traditional rural pursuits, as well as the state-run shows. According to Lady Wilde, in the Aran Islands it was the custom to sacrifice a black cock in honour of the saint and fix large crosses made of straw or flowers on the door post. (At

St Patrick's Day in Dublin

The St Patrick's Day parade in Dublin is now a huge global gathering celebrating every and any connection to Ireland.

other times of the year, sacrificial animals included an ox at Christmas, lamb at Easter, and a goose on St Michael's Day, or Michaelmas, on 29 September to mark the harvest.)

In the nineteenth century, a small cardboard or silk disc of intersecting crosses known as a *croiseog* was made in honour of St Patrick, especially by children. It was worn on the chest, and sometimes the child decorated the cross with real blood by pricking his or her own finger. However, this custom eventually died out and the wearing of the *croiseog* was replaced by the wearing of shamrock, ribbon or harp in the twentieth century, and by football jerseys and green headgear in the twenty-first!

DID YOU KNOW?

On St Patrick's Day in 2012 the town of Bandon in County Cork broke the world record for the largest number dressed as leprechauns, with 1,263 people taking part.

ITALY

The Pozzo di San Patrizio (St Patrick's Well) is in Orvieto, Umbria. Its construction began in 1527 when the Holy Roman Emperor Charles V sacked Rome, and the pope, Clement VII who had fled there, was trying to protect the city's water supply in the event of a siege. Remarkably, at the time, the name was inspired by legends that Patrick's Purgatory in Lough Derg, County Donegal, was an entrance to the Underworld, or to Purgatory.

NIGERIA

Because of missionary work in Nigeria, particularly by the St Patrick's Missionary Society, Irish bishops there influenced the choice of patron saint after independence in 1960. Patrick became the country's patron in 1961, the same year Ireland opened its embassy in Lagos. Nigeria also has the distinction of drinking more Guinness per capita than anywhere outside Ireland.

The St Patrick's Missionary Society was founded on 17 March 1932 by Monsignor Patrick Whitney at Kiltegan, County Wicklow. Its stated aim was the evangelisation of Nigeria and beyond. The missionaries worked in Cameroon, Kenya, Malawi, South Africa, South Sudan, Uganda, Zambia and Zimbabwe. They also went to South America. Nigerian Catholics now number some twenty million – more than five times the number in Ireland. However, the success of the mission has been overshadowed by the criminal abuse of children that some missionaries were guilty of, and the Society has been forced to pay out hundreds of thousands of euros in compensation.

SCOTLAND

The country that is today known as Scotland has a special relationship with Ireland. It was half-ignored by the Romans, but was very much on the minds of Irish tribes who came and settled the Highlands from the fifth century. The closest sea crossing between Ireland and Britain is a mere 19 kilometres (12 miles) and so there were always many links between Ulster and western Scotland. The Irish tribe, the Dál Riada, for example, were particularly attracted to the area.

On the north bank of the River Clyde in Clydesdale, in the southerly Grampian Mountains, there is an ancient parish called Old, or West, Kilpatrick. This, local tradition has it, is the real birthplace of Patrick. There were special rocks associated with him, and enough of a tradition in the area for medieval pilgrims to come to the church of St Patrick in Kilpatrick, beside which there was a holy well (now closed). Although this well was linked with him from the earliest times, it was not until the 1930s it was officially named after the saint in order to promote tourism to the area. Unlike most holy wells, Old Kilpatrick's holy well was actually manmade. The Romans were the first to sink it to provide water, before Patrick's time, when they were still considering conquering the region. Another link between Patrick and Scotland is the *Letter to Coroticus*. In the fifth century King Coroticus's territory extended over part of the River Clyde and western coastal regions, known later as Strathclyde. He was a Christian, but was not above kidnapping and selling other Christians into slavery. In retaliation Patrick wrote a blistering letter, designed to be read aloud for maximum humiliation, in which he excommunicated Coroticus. According to Muirchú, on hearing of this, Coroticus turned into a fox and raced away, never to be seen again.

ST PATRICK'S CATHEDRALS AROUND THE WORLD

According to a well-known Catholic website, catholic.org, there are more than 870 Catholic churches worldwide named for Patrick, but it's likely there are even more than that. As well as churches worldwide, which were often founded by Irish clergy dispensing both the Gospel and a Catholic education, today there are also St Patrick's cathedrals and basilicas in many places including:

Auckland in New Zealand, Fremantle in Western Australia,

Ballarat and Melbourne in Victoria, Parramatta in New South Wales, Pune and Gumla in India, Karachi in Pakistan, Connecticut, Montana, Ottawa, New Jersey, New York, North Carolina, Pennsylvania and Texas in the US, and the provinces of Quebec, Ontario and Newfoundland and Labrador in Canada.

GOING GREEN

Of all the consequences of the posthumous popularity of Patrick, few could have predicted this: the green illumination of the world's most famous landmarks to celebrate St Patrick's Day.

The Global Greening initiative started casually in 2010 with one of Tourism Ireland's employees in Australia approaching the Sydney Opera House and using its existing lighting system to turn it green for St Patrick's Day. Just over one in three Australians is of Irish descent, so seeing their most famous landmark turn green delighted many. From there the idea snowballed and Tourism Ireland persuaded more and more countries to take part.

This satirical cartoon shows how important Ireland is to Irish-Americans on St Patrick's Day, 1911.

Sydney Opera House, gone green for St Patrick's Day

The stated aim of this initiative is to bring a smile to people's faces – and to promote Ireland as a tourist destination at the same time. Of course, the USA is an enthusiastic participant in this initiative. Regular sites here include Niagara Falls, on both the Canadian and American sides, Chicago's Civic Opera House and City Hall San Francisco. The iconic Empire State Building in New York has unilaterally gone green to celebrate St Patrick's Day since the 1990s. It also goes red, blue and white to mark other festivals, reflecting the city's famous diversity. In South America, the world-famous Christ the Redeemer statue, which towers over Rio De Janeiro, Brazil, also goes green.

Traditional European markets for tourism to Ireland include Italy, Germany, Britain and France. Regular recognisable participants from these countries include Rome's Colosseum, the Leaning Tower of Pisa, the London Eye, Paris Disneyland's

Niagara Falls going green on both sides of the USA-Canada border

The iconic Christ the Redeemer statue, Rio de Janeiro, Brazil

The London Eye, England

The Colosseum, Rome, Italy

Sleeping Beauty Palace and Munich's Olympic Tower, to name but a few. At home in Ireland the illuminated buildings have included Dublin's GPO, the Four Courts, Kilmainham, Áras an Uachtaráin, the Rock of Cashel, and a number of medieval castles.

Today, Tourism Ireland has a close eye on emerging markets, including India and China. In a major coup for the initiative, even the Great Wall of China, a UNESCO world heritage site, regularly turns itself into the Green Wall of China for St Patrick's Day. By 2014, the number of participating sites exceeded one hundred for the first time. By 2018 participants numbered more than two hundred – and the list keeps growing.

There is a seam of quirkiness running through the initiative; it isn't just famous monuments that have had the green treatment.

The Great Wall of China

One year, St Patrick's Day fell on the day of Sweden's bandy final (bandy is a game on ice resembling hockey), and Stockholm's Friends Arena turned green to celebrate. Another year, Kenya participated by green-lighting a lion statue made entirely of recycled rubber and plastic waste. Other unconventional participants over the years have included a herd of elephants, a team of ice swimmers in Finland, a London museum's famous blue whale skeleton and a solitary Canadian goat!

A FESTIVAL FOR EVERYONE

It is fair to say that the Global Greening initiative is quintessentially Irish in its outlook: good-humoured and inventive. It welcomes such a wide variety of participants because it reflects the diverse outlook of modern Ireland.

Ireland and being Irish is no longer exclusively associated with being white, or being religious. There are myriad ways to enjoy Irishness, and the ancient festival of St Patrick's Day has proven this by becoming a celebration for everyone, everywhere.

SELECT
BIBLIOGRAPHY

BOOKS, JOURNALS AND ARTICLES

Bury, JB (2010), *The Life and World of Ireland's Saint*, London; New York: Tauris Parke Paperbacks.

Bury, JB (1905), *The Life of St Patrick and His Place in History*, London: Macmillan & Co.

Bhreathnach, E (2014), Ireland in the Medieval World, AD 400–1000: *Landscape, Kingship and Religion, Dublin*: Four Courts Press.

Cahill, T (1995), *How the Irish Saved Civilisation*, London: Hodder.

Clydesdale District Libraries and Museums Dept (1893), T*he History of the Parish of West or Old Kilpatrick*.

Corfe, T (1973), *Saint Patrick and Irish Christianity*, London: Cambridge University Press.

Cronin, M and Adair, D (2002), *The Wearing of the Green: A History of St Patrick's Day*, London: Routledge.

Cusack, MF (1871), *The Life of Saint Patrick, Apostle of Ireland*, London: Longmans, Green & Co.

De Breffny, B (1982), *In the Steps of St Patrick,* London: Thames and Hudson.

De Paor, L (1993), *St Patrick's World*, Dublin: Four Courts Press.

De Vere, A (1872), *The Legend of St Patrick*, London: Henry S King and Co.

De Vinne, D (1870), *History of the Irish Primitive Church*, New York: Francis Hart & Co.

Doherty, C (1995), '*The problem of Patrick*' in History Ireland, Vol. 3, No. 1, Spring.

Fulton Hope, A (1892), *The Conversion of the Teutonic Race*, London: Burns and Oates.

Gallico, P (1967) *The Steadfast Man*, London: New English Library.

Grattan-Flood, William (1908), '*St. Darerca*' in The Catholic Encyclopedia Vol. 4, New York: Robert Appleton Company.

Gregory, Lady A (1904), '*Oisín and St Patrick*', in Gods and Fighting Men, London: John Murray.

Hoagland, K ed. (1947), *1000 Years of Irish Poetry*, New York: The Devin-Adair Company.

Hughes, H (2010), *Croagh Patrick*, Dublin: The O'Brien Press.

Hyde, Dr D (1899), *Literary History of Ireland*, London: T Fisher Unwin

Keogh, R (1997), 'Escape from the mountain' in *History Ireland*, Vol 5, No 1, Spring.

Letts, WM (1932), *St Patrick: The Travelling Man*, London: Ivor Nicholson and Watson Ltd.

Lewis, S (1840), T*opographical Dictionary*, London: S Lewis & Co.

Luce, JV, and Losack, M (2015), *The Letters of Saint Patrick*, Annamoe: Céile Dé.

Maguire, JF (1868), *The Irish in America, by John Francis Maguire MP*, New York: D & J Sadlier & Co.

MacNeill, E (1924), 'The Fifteenth Centenary of Saint Patrick: A Suggested Form of Commemoration' in *Studies, An Irish*

Quarterly Review, Vol. 13, No. 50 (June), 181–182.

McCormack, J (2008), *St Patrick: The Real Story, As Told in His Own Words*, Columba Press.

McDonnell, H (2007), *St Patrick: His Life and Legend*, Glastonbury: Wooden Books.

McGee, T D'Arcy (1883), *The Poems of Thomas D'Arcy McGee*, New York: D & J Sadlier.

Michaud, M-C (2008), 'The Saint Patrick's Day Celebration in New York since 2000: An Ethnic Festival Revisited by the *New York Times*' in *Études irlandaises année*, Vol. 33, No. 1, 115–133.

Mooney, J (1889), 'The Holiday Customs of Ireland' in *Proceedings of the American Philosophical Society*, Vol. 26 No. 130, 377–427, http://www.jstor.org/stable/983181, accessed June 2018.

O'Farrell, P (2005), *Irish Blessings, Toasts & Curses*, Cork: Mercier Press.

O'Grady, S Hayes, trans. (1892), 'The Colloquy with the Ancients' in *Silva Gadelica*, London: Williams and Norgate.

O'Longan, J and Gilbert JJ, eds. (1876), *Leabhar Breac Facsimile*, Dublin: Royal Irish Academy.

O'Rahilly, TF (1942), *The Two Patricks: A Lecture on the History of Christianity in Fifth-century Ireland*, Dublin Institute for Advanced Studies.

Simms, GO (2004), *Saint Patrick: Ireland's Patron Saint*, Dublin: The O'Brien Press.

Winn, C (2006), *I Never Knew That about Ireland*, London: Ebury Digital.

Wilde, Lady J (1887), *Ancient Legends, Mystic Charms and*

Superstitions of Ireland. London: Ward and Downey.

SONGS AND POEMS

Seabrook, AJ (1911), *Irish-American Patriotic Songs*, Chicago: AJ Seabrook

'St Patrick, One Day, Came Up Bantry Bay', 'The Arrival of St Patrick' and 'The Monks of the Screw' in *Blarney Comic Songbook*, Glasgow: Cameron and Ferguson, year unknown.

'Hymn on the Life of St Patrick' (1868) in *The Ecclesiastical Record*. Anonymous translation.

WEBSITES

'A Hymn on the Life, Virtues, and Miracles of St Patrick, Composed by his disciple, St Fiech, Bishop of Sletty', http://www.gutenberg.org/files/39428/39428-h/39428-h.htm, accessed 7 November 2016.

'Autumnal Rambles about New Quay, County Clare: No. 5 St Patrick's Well', http://www.clarelibrary.ie/eolas/coclare/history/autumnal_rambles/stpatricks_well.htm, accessed August 2016.

'Annagh-Killadangan Archaeological Complex', http://www.clewbaytrail.com/show.php?SitesID=5, accessed November 2016.

Battersby, Eileen, 'Following the Clew Trail', http://www.irishtimes.com/culture/following-the-clew-trail-1.368669, Wednesday, 6 August, 2003, accessed December 2017.

'*The Confessio*', https://www.confessio.ie/etexts/confessio_english#01

Catholic Directory, http://www.thecatholicdirectory.com/

directory.cfm?whichtab=2, accessed November 2018.

'Fulacht fiadh', http://moylough.galwaycommunityheritage.
org/content/places/fulacht-fiadh-lakeview-lake, accessed
August 2016.

'Glaspatrick Church', http://www.clewbaytrail.com/show.
php?SitesID=9, accessed November 2016.

'Church Ruins', http://www.limerickdioceseheritage.org/
ShanagoldenFoynes.htm, accessed August 2016.

'Traces of St Patrick in Ballina, History of Co. Mayo', http://
www.mayo-ireland.ie/en/about-mayo/history/saint-patrick-
ballina.html, accessed December 2017.

'Holy wells', http://holywell.seomraranga.com/
holywellsireland.htm, accessed January 2018.

'St Patrick's Chair, Marown, Isle Of Man', https://
thejournalofantiquities.com/2013/06/02/st-patricks-chair-
marown-isle-of-man/, accessed June 2017.

ILLUSTRATIONS

The author and publisher would like to thank the following for permission to use photographs and illustrations:

Pages 68, 82, 88 and 99 © David Rooney; pages 42, 51, 76–77 © Harry Hughes; pages 22, 33, 34, 52, 70, 149, 154, 166, 167, 172, 175, 180 and 189 © Library of Congress Prints and Photographs Division; pages 102, 114, 125, 126, 127, 128, 129, 130 and 133 © Marian Broderick; page 55 © National Museum of Ireland; page 36 © Newry, Mourne and Down District Council via Tourism Northern Ireland; pages 69 and 86 © The O'Brien Press; pages 8, 15, 20–21, 27, 30, 39, 47, 49, 59, 60, 64, 65, 66, 78, 100–101, 107, 109, 111, 115, 117, 124, 136, 143, 146, 148, 168, 170, 174, 177, 178, 179, 182 and 184 © Shutterstock; page 185 © Tourism Ireland; pages 162–163, 164, 190, 191, 192 and 193 © Tourism Ireland's Global Greening; pages 72, 73, 75 and 105 © Tourism Northern Ireland; page 113 © Tyrone and Sperrins destination via Tourism Northern Ireland.

If any involuntary infringement of copyright has occurred, sincere apologies are offered, and the owners of such copyright are requested to contact the publisher.

INDEX OF PLACE NAMES

A

Aghagower, County Mayo 127

Altadaven, County Tyrone 112

Aran Islands 184

Ardfert, County Kerry 37

Armagh 71–74, 104

Australia 178–179

B

Balla, County Mayo 126

Ballina, County Mayo 133

Ballintubber, County Mayo 123

Belcoo, County Fermanagh, *see* Holywell

Benbulben, County Sligo 49

Boheh Stone, Lankill, County Mayo 132

Boyne, River 32, 141

C

Canada 179–180

Carrigatogher, County Tipperary 38

Cashel, County Tipperary 153–155

Clogher, County Tyrone 112

Clonmel, County Tipperary 38

Coleraine, County Derry-Londonderry 115

Croagh Patrick, County Mayo 50–54

Croghan Hill, County Offaly 38

D

Downpatrick, County Down 108
Downpatrick Head, County Mayo 136–139
Dublin 148–149
Duff, River 139
Duncrun, County Derry-Londonderry 40

E

England 180–181

F

Foghill, County Mayo 40, 135
France 13, 14, 17, 181–182

G

Glaspatrick, County Mayo 40
Grianán of Aileach, County Donegal 116

H

Holywell, Belcoo, County Fermanagh 113

I

Inver Dé, County Wicklow 141
Inishowen, County Donegal 118
Ireland, Northern, *see* Northern Ireland
Ireland, Republic of 116–157, 183–185
Isle of Man 182

Italy 186

K
Kenya 194
Kildare 147
Kill na Greina, County Cork 41
Kilgeever, County Mayo 41
Killala, County Mayo 134
Killeter, County Tyrone 41
Killycluggin, County Cavan 121
Knockpatrick, County Limerick 157

L
Lough Derg, County Donegal 118

M
Magherakeel, County Tyrone 43
Moy, River 133
Mungret, County Limerick 43
Murrisk, County Mayo 131

N
Newry, County Down 104
Nigeria 186
Northern Ireland 104–115

R
Raholp, County Down 110
Rathcroghan, County Roscommon 140

S

St Patrick's Trail, County Antrim 104
St Patrick's Way Pilgrim Walk 104
Saul, County Down 106
Scotland 187–188
Shannon, River 31
Skerries, County Dublin 148
Slane, County Meath 58–61
Slemish Mountain, County Antrim 104–106
Slieve Donard, County Down 48, 49
Slievenamon, County Tipperary 156
Slieve Patrick, County Down 112
Straffan, County Kildare 43
Struell Wells, County Down 110
Sweden 194

T

Tara, County Meath 61–65
Tawnagh West, County Clare 44
Tobberpatrick, Portstewart, County Derry-Londonderry 44
Tóchar Phádraig, County Mayo 122
Trinity College, Dublin 44
Tullaghan, County Leitrim 44

U

Uisneach, Hill of, County Westmeath 143–145
USA 165–177
    Arkansas 169
    Boston, MA 168

Georgetown, WA 176

Los Angeles, CA 176

New York City, NY 171–174, 176

Pennsylvania 176

V

Vartry, River 142

W

Wicklow, County Wicklow 141